CAMBRIDGE NAVAL AND MILITARY SERIES

GENERAL EDITORS
SIR JULIAN S. CORBETT, LL. M., F.S.A.
H. J. EDWARDS, C.B., C.B.E., M.A.

T0381936

LORD HOOD AND THE
DEFENCE OF TOULON

THE FIRST VISCOUNT HOOD

LORD HOOD
AND THE
DEFENCE OF TOULON

BY

J. HOLLAND ROSE, Litt.D.

VERE HARMSWORTH PROFESSOR OF NAVAL HISTORY, UNIVERSITY OF
CAMBRIDGE; HON. LITT.D. UNIVERSITY OF MANCHESTER;
HON. LL.D. UNIVERSITY OF NEBRASKA AND OF
AMHERST COLLEGE (MASS.)

CAMBRIDGE
AT THE UNIVERSITY PRESS
1922

CAMBRIDGE
UNIVERSITY PRESS

University Printing House, Cambridge CB2 8BS, United Kingdom

Published in the United States of America by Cambridge University Press, New York

Cambridge University Press is part of the University of Cambridge.

It furthers the University's mission by disseminating knowledge in the pursuit of education, learning and research at the highest international levels of excellence.

www.cambridge.org
Information on this title: www.cambridge.org/9781107419094

© Cambridge University Press 1922

First published 1922
First paperback edition 2014

A catalogue record for this publication is available from the British Library

ISBN 978-1-107-41909-4 Paperback

PREFACE

THE events at Toulon in 1793 have often been described from the side of Bonaparte, whose career they so brilliantly inaugurated. But they have not been recounted adequately from the standpoint of the defenders. To do so, especially as regards Lord Hood and the British naval forces, is the purpose of this volume, which aims at exhibiting the defence of Toulon as an outcome of British policy in the Mediterranean and as an important episode of the Revolutionary War. The interest of the theme is enhanced by the fact that Nelson, Elphinstone (Lord Keith), Linzee, Tyler, Byam Martin, and other eminent naval officers, together with Thomas Graham of Balgowan (Lord Lynedoch), Lord Mulgrave, Generals O'Hara and David Dundas, took part in the operations; while our ambassadors and envoys, Lord St Helens at Madrid, Sir Morton Eden at Vienna, Sir William Hamilton at Naples, John Hampden Trevor at Turin and Francis Drake at Genoa, worked strenuously to assure the despatch of troops or supplies to Hood's hard pressed force.

Their efforts are set forth in the numerous despatches published in the Appendices; and their failure throws up in lurid light the selfishness and slackness which were the bane of the First Coalition. In general I have printed in full only new materials. Some other despatches have been published by M. Cottin in his works, *Toulon et les Anglais* and *Toulon et les Princes*. These I have either described in the text, with due acknowledgment, or have summarized in the Appendices. I have also omitted or summarized the long despatches of Lord Mulgrave which appeared in the *London Gazette*, and others of a more general character published in the *Annual Register* (1793), the *Naval Chronicle* (1799), *The Life and*

Letters of Sir Gilbert Elliot, the *Life of Sir Sidney Smith,* and *The Dropmore Papers.*

My thanks are due to Viscount Hood for very kindly permitting me to publish many new letters of the first Viscount Hood, which are in his possession, also to reproduce the engraving which appears as frontispiece. I am greatly indebted to Mr A. B. Hinds, M.A., formerly Student of Christchurch, Oxford, for valued help both in the collection of materials, especially at the archives of Turin and Venice, and in advice and criticism while the work was in progress. I also cordially thank M. Arthur Chuquet, and his publisher, M. Armand Colin, for permission to adapt the plan of Toulon in his work *La Jeunesse de Napoléon* (Toulon). It may be stated here that the account of events at Toulon given by Moreau de Jonnès in his *Mémoires,* recently translated by Brigadier-General A. J. Abdy (J. Murray, 1920), abounds in inaccuracies, some of which are noted at the end of Chapter V of this work.

J. H. R.

CAMBRIDGE,
    December, 1921.

CONTENTS

*also available for download from www.cambridge.org/9781107419094

LIST OF ABBREVIATIONS

Adm. Med.   = Admiralty Despatches relating to the Mediterranean.

Ann. Reg.   = *Annual Register.*

Auckland Journal = *Journal and Correspondence of Lord Auckland*, vol. II (1861).

Chevalier   = E. Chevalier, *Hist. de la Marine française sous la première République* (Paris, 1888).

Chuquet   = A. Chuquet, *La Jeunesse de Napoléon* (Toulon), Paris, 1899.

Cottin   = P. Cottin, *Toulon et les Anglais en 1793* (Paris, 1898).

Dropmore P.   = *The MSS. of J. B. Fortescue Esq. preserved at Dropmore* (Historical MSS. Commission, 1894).

Elliot, Life   = *Life and Letters of Sir Gilbert Elliot, first Earl of Minto* (1874).

F.O. Austria, etc. = Foreign Office despatches relating to Austria, etc.

Fortescue   = Hon. J. W. Fortescue, *History of the British Army* (esp. vol. IV, Pt. I), (1915).

Fox   = C. J. Fox, *Napoleon and the Siege of Toulon* (Washington, 1902).

H.O.   = Home Office despatches relating to military and naval affairs in the Mediterranean.

James   = W. James, *The Naval History of Great Britain* (1793–1830), vol. I.

Jomini   = Jomini, *Guerres de la Révolution*, 15 vols. (Paris, 1820).

Mahan   = A. T. Mahan, *Influence of Sea Power upon the Fr. Rev. and Empire* (2 vols., London, 1893).

Nicolas   = Sir N. Harris Nicolas, *Letters and Despatches of Lord Nelson*, vol. I (1845).

N.R.S.   = Navy Records Society.

Pons   = Pons, *Mémoires...de Toulon* (Paris, 1825).

Revel   = Thaon de Revel, *Méms. sur la Guerre des Alpes* (Turin, 1871).

Sorel   = A. Sorel, *L'Europe et la Révolution française*, Pt. III (Paris, 1897).

CHAPTER I

THE EUROPEAN BACKGROUND

WHEN the development of the stronghold and dockyard of Toulon enabled the French fleet to command the Mediterranean, British statesmen and seamen, during their frequent wars with France, sought for the means to thwart that domination. Accordingly, from the reign of William III onwards, the maintenance of the British fleet in that sea became one of the master aims of naval strategy. By the capture of Gibraltar in 1704 and of Minorca four years later, we were in a position effectively to counteract French efforts in that quarter, with the result that Anglo-French struggles, which had previously centred in home waters, extended to the great inland sea. This expansion of effort was due mainly to the following reasons. French statesmen found in the Toulon fleet a powerful weapon for coercing Spain and the Italian States; while, on the contrary, we sought to foil their efforts. Also, if no very pressing duties detained the Toulon fleet in the Mediterranean, French seamen sought as soon as possible to unite it with their Atlantic squadrons in order to overpower the British navy; while sound strategy impelled us to prevent such union. Hence, though war generally arose between the two Powers out of Netherlandish or colonial disputes, yet it tended to be fought out largely in the Mediterranean. The Revolutionary War formed no exception to this rule. Indeed, the transference of naval strife to that sea, especially in and after 1798, was destined to exert a curiously warping influence on the character of the war, assimilating it more and more to the age-long struggles for colonial supremacy or for the control of the Netherlands.

The latter motive was prominent among the causes that conduced to the declaration of war by the French Republic on Great Britain and Holland on February 1, 1793. But, so soon as the safety of Dutch territory was assured, British aims turned southwards. Action in the Mediterranean was commanded both by the general considerations above noted and by the requirements of our allies. French aggression brought us into line with a powerful coalition. Austria, Prussia and Sardinia, it is true, had in the autumn of 1792 suffered sharp reverses at the hands of the French Republicans, the Sardinians being driven from their County of Nice by a French army which had the support of the Toulon fleet; and further misfortunes threatened them on the Italian Riviera unless a British fleet came to their assistance[1]. Another reason for its arrival was the protection of the kingdom of Naples, whose Government late in 1792 had been coerced by the apparition of a powerful squadron from Toulon. But, besides the rescue of Sardinia and South Italy, wider motives were operative. The French Republic having in March 1793 declared war on Spain, hostilities soon began on the Pyrenean border; and the Spaniards desired the assistance of British warships for the projected invasion of Roussillon. In short the supremacy of the Union flag in the Mediterranean would serve to hearten the weaker States of the Coalition and bind them together for an offensive against the south of France.

The situation somewhat resembled that which prompted one of the grandest designs of Marlborough. The victor of Blenheim and Ramillies, not content with driving the French from the Rhineland and Flanders, sought to deal them a homethrust by the capture of Toulon. Relying on the alliance of the Emperor and the Duke of Savoy, he in 1707 planned an expedition which affords one of the first examples, on a great scale, of conjoint naval and military operations. Prince Eugène, crossing the Maritime Alps, was to advance quickly through the County of Nice towards Toulon and with the aid of a powerful British fleet capture that stronghold and destroy French naval power in the Mediterranean. For reasons that need not be stated here, the plan miscarried; but it came so near to success as to lead the French governor of Toulon to sink the fleet which was one of the chief objects of the Allies.

In the spring and summer of 1793 the omens seemed more propitious than in 1707. The six allies now in arms against France were stronger, and, to all appearance, she was weaker, than in the reign of Louis XIV. In the north the fortresses erected by

---

[1] Jomini, II, 198; Chevalier, p. 38.

Vauban alone stayed their onset; in the west the Royalist peasants routed the Republicans; and large parts of the south and centre cast off the yoke of the Jacobins now supreme at Paris. The men of Marseilles and Toulon declared for a moderate Republic far different from that of the Terrorists. Therefore, as the summer advanced, another reason for British action in the Mediterranean became apparent, viz. co-operation with the moderates and Royalists of the south of France. This motive, as will duly appear, finds no place in the instructions issued to Lord Hood. His objective was Toulon and the French Mediterranean fleet, then consisting of sixteen sail-of-the-line.

On no side did the Jacobinical Republic betray signs of nervousness or apprehension. Its aggressiveness in adding Great Britain, Holland and Spain to the ranks of the Coalition harmonized with its strategy, which betokened confidence, even defiance. The Jacobins had good cause not to despair. France possessed the enormous advantage of the central position, which conferred the power of striking swiftly against the Allied forces thinly spread out over a wide circumference; and this advantage was utilized to the full by the geometrical genius of Carnot, "the organizer of victory." Moreover, her enemies were severed not merely by distance but by diversities of aim. The invaders all cherished plans of "indemnification" which tended to sunder them and to unite her in an increasingly solid resistance[1]. Their French sympathizers were also rent by incurable schisms. The French malcontents included "pure" Royalists, who sought to bring back *l'ancien régime*, constitutionalists who desired the limited monarchy of 1791, and moderate or more advanced Republicans. These parties cherished bitter animosities, so that Lord Mulgrave, commander of the Allied troops at Toulon, wrote thus to our envoy at Turin:

You must not send us one *émigré* of any sort; they would be a nuisance; they are all so various and so violent, whether for despotism, constitution or Republic, that we should be distracted with their quarrels; and they are so assuming, forward, dictatorial and full of complaints, that no business could go on with them. Lord Hood is averse to receiving any of them[2].

[1] For the war in Flanders see Fortescue, IV, Pt. I, chs. 4, 5.
[2] F.O. Sardinia, 13, Mulgrave to Trevor, Oct. 19.

On the other hand, up to the end of 1793, the Jacobins were of one mind; they controlled the machinery of government, and had on their side the instinct of obedience to the central authority instilled by ages of centralized rule, and now quickened by enthusiasm for democracy and hatred of the monarchical invaders. Resistance to the Jacobins spelt treason to the Republic and treason to *la patrie*. Above all, the Parisian Government acted with immense energy. The Committee of Public Safety acquired new vigour by the entry of Robespierre on July 26 and of Carnot on August 10. On August 23 it obtained from the now subservient National Convention a decree enforcing conscription in all but name, by subjecting every adult Frenchman to some form of national service. A *levée en masse* was decreed, and its effects were to be seen in the hordes of eager though ill-disciplined troops which in the autumn of 1793 crushed internal revolts and beat back the Allies on the frontiers.

While France was girding herself with new and hitherto undreamt of strength, the Allies waged the campaign in a manner which revealed the inner divergence of their aims. Austria and Prussia were on very bad terms owing to the Second Partition of Poland recently carried out by Russia and Prussia to the exclusion of the Habsburg Power. By way of compensation Austria proposed to revive her old scheme of annexing Bavaria, indemnifying the Elector by assigning to him either her Belgic lands, or (when Great Britain objected to this) certain provinces conquered from France—either the north of France down to the River Somme, or Alsace-Lorraine. When news of this scheme leaked out, Prussia, gorged with the spoils of Poland, showed little desire for continuing the war against France. The Habsburgs, furious at being duped in the Polish affair, sought to hold their unwilling Prussian allies to the compact of February 7, 1792, whereby they promised to work together in the settlement of French affairs. But the Coalition was in danger of collapse, and probably would have fallen asunder but for the diplomatic, financial and naval succours forthcoming from Great Britain. Yet, as she had recently been on bad terms with Spain, Prussia and Austria, she was ill fitted to be, what she soon became, the leader of the Coalition. Her compacts of 1788 with Prussia and the Dutch Republic still subsisted, but intrigues at Berlin and timidity at the Hague atrophied that union. In truth, she was on cordial terms only with Sardinia and Naples, who urgently needed her naval protection.

At sea she was strong. Parsimonious to the army, Pitt had granted money liberally and wisely to the navy; and, assisted by that able comptroller, Sir Charles Middleton (afterwards Lord Barham), he raised the grand total of sail-of-the-line to 115, there being also 135 smaller vessels available. It is probable that the French Revolutionists, puffed up with their military triumphs in 1792, reckoned on winning the war on land before this mighty array could be adequately equipped. This notion was not altogether chimerical; for owing to the wholesale discharges of seamen in 1783, nothing but the relentless work of the press gang would avail to man so great a fleet. At first, the opinion prevailed that the strain on the navy would not be severe; for Great Britain figured merely as an auxiliary to a mighty coalition. French commerce also having been ruined during the Revolution, there was little prospect of the copious prize money which in former wars had quickened the recruiting for the fleet; and the high bounties now offered for the army diverted men to the junior service. Such were the later statements of the second Earl of Chatham, First Lord of the Admiralty; but he claimed that, despite these disadvantages, the navy secured the unexampled increase of 56,337 men in the first year of war[1]. Nevertheless in the first months the scarcity of men was severely felt. Even in September 1793 the Marquis of Buckingham congratulated Lord Grenville on the arrival of the East and West India convoys, which would yield at least 2000 pressed men; "and God knows your fleet wants them[2]."

The urgent need of naval assistance to Sardinia and Naples explains the readiness with which those States made treaties with the Court of St James's. Austria and Spain also pressed for the dispatch of Hood's fleet; for though a Spanish fleet, under Don Borja, put to sea and captured a French frigate and 1225 troops left by the French on the St Pierre Isles off the Isle of Sardinia,

---

[1] Undated Mem. for the King in Chatham MSS.
[2] *Dropmore P.*, II, 443; *Letters of Sir T. Byam Martin* (N.R.S.), III, 380–2.

yet the outbreak of pestilence on board soon compelled it to return to Carthagena in a deplorable state[1]; and, when Hood was delayed by causes soon to be explained, certain Francophils at Madrid angrily exclaimed that England purposely postponed his departure in order to expose the Spanish marine to destruction. Lord St Helens, our ambassador at Madrid, thus described the situation in a "private" letter to Lord Grenville, written on May 29, four days after the signature of the Anglo-Spanish treaty of alliance at Aranjuez:

...The truth is that it is hardly possible to obtain anything from these people but through the medium of their fears, so that they are infinitely more untractable and difficult to deal with as friends than as enemies. Our chief antagonist is the Minister of Marine, M. Valdès, who, in common with but too many other persons, has persuaded himself that the secret aim of Great Britain in the present war is to engage the French and Spaniards to batter each other's ships to pieces and so secure to herself in future an uncontested superiority over both; for which reason, added to an ill-judged demency, he is sure to oppose every plan which he thinks may lead the Spanish Navy into any service of danger.

He added that the chief minister Godoy, Duke of Alcudia, would through ignorance be probably misled by Valdès, and that British officers, when they arrived, must be extremely careful not to offend the Spaniards[2]. The dispute concerning Nootka Sound in what was soon to be called Vancouver Island was designedly kept open by the Spanish Government, which also displayed extreme jealousy as to the extension of British trade and influence in the Mediterranean.

It follows, then, that our union was cordial only with the hard-pressed kingdoms of Sardinia and Naples. The treaty which, on April 25, our Foreign Secretary, Lord Grenville, signed with Sardinia bound her to maintain in the field an army of 50,000 men, she receiving in return an annual subsidy of £200,000 and support from a British fleet. The two States mutually guaranteed their territories—a clause which, for us, implied an engagement to recover Savoy and Nice for King Victor Amadeus (a promise

---

[1] Duro, *Armada española*, VIII, 32. Lord St Helens on July 19 (F.O. Spain, 27) reported 3500 sick landed at Carthagena. The Venetian ambassador reported over 300 dead and 3332 sick (Venetian Archives, *Spain*, vol. 189).
[2] F.O. Spain, 27.

not fulfilled until 1814). By the Anglo-Spanish treaty of May 25 the two Powers promised to oppose France, and to seek to prevent neutrals from helping her trade; also each agreed to convoy the merchantmen of its ally. The convention with Naples, signed there on July 12 by Sir William Hamilton and General Acton, bound that Court to make common cause against France, to assist the British forces in the Mediterranean with a body of 6000 troops, four sail-of-the-line and eight smaller craft, provided that Great Britain would maintain in that sea *une flotte respectable*, establish naval supremacy, pay for the transport and upkeep of the said contingent, and protect Neapolitan commerce at sea.

Finally, the British treaty of July 14 with Prussia, and that of August 30 with the Emperor, implied little more than a loose union against France. At that time, too, Austro-Prussian rivalry was so acute that all the efforts of Great Britain to secure vigorous action in the common cause proved fruitless. Not until September 24 did Francis consent to detach from the troops in his Milanese province 5000 men for service at Toulon. The sequel will show how that promise was kept[1].

Meanwhile the Jacobins were mustering forces with a view to an offensive in Flanders, the Rhineland, the Maritime Alps and the Pyrenees. Nay! They were preparing to strike blows in the Mediterranean. On June 22 and 24 the French Convention passed decrees which augured vigorous action; they placed an embargo on all merchantmen in order speedily to man the Toulon fleet and reinforced it by eight sail-of-the-line from Brest and Rochefort[2]. Thenceforth the need for the assertion of British supremacy in that sea became urgent, all the more so as the chief food supplies for the French armies about to invade North Italy came by sea from Genoa and Leghorn[3].

[1] F.O. Austria, 34, Eden to Grenville, Aug. 31, Sept. 25.
[2] Lévy-Schneider, *Jean Bon St André*, p. 415.
[3] The despatches of Trevor at Turin, of Lord Hervey, the British envoy at Florence, and of Brame, our consul at Genoa, teem with complaints as to the flagrant manner in which the corn ships of Genoa and Leghorn supplied the French armies. On April 10 Trevor stated that Genoa had sold corn so lavishly to France as to produce a scarcity at that city; and on the 20th he reported the sailing of eleven or twelve corn ships for Toulon or Marseilles. French frigates had recently attacked Oneglia because from that Sardinian port privateers set out to intercept that trade, which the presence of Hood alone could terminate. Even on August 27, *i.e.* five weeks

The diversion of a powerful fleet to the Mediterranean early in the war has been criticized as involving an unwarrantable dispersion of force. But the reasons in its favour have now been shown to be unanswerably cogent. Within six weeks of Hood's arrival fortune conferred on the Allies an almost fantastic boon. In truth their admission into Toulon at the end of August 1793 ought to have dealt a mortal blow to the French Republic. No event of the war (so wrote Drake to Grenville on September 12) has so much tended to bring about a safe and honourable peace[1]. Such was the belief at the Allied capitals; and that excess of confidence was part reason for the discreditable failure. The story of Toulon in 1793 is concerned with an expedition suddenly confronted with an immense but unforeseen opportunity; it describes efforts courageously extemporized on the spot but never adequately supported from home; it deals with Allies who were skilful in promoting friction and in shirking or postponing disagreeable duties until the occasion had vanished. It tells also of a raw Administration gathering strength from despair, enforcing national unity even in the midst of schism, and developing efficiency out of apparently hopeless turmoil.

after Hood's arrival, Francis Drake, British minister at Genoa, reported that British cruisers had not wholly stopped the trade, and that of the 30,000 quarters of corn still in Genoa most had been bought by the French, and the leading families of Genoa profited so much by the sales of corn that the authorities would try to get it through. F.O. Sardinia, 11; F.O. Genoa, 6.

[1] F.O. Genoa, 6.

CHAPTER II

THE OCCUPATION OF TOULON

VICE-ADMIRAL, first Viscount Hood, who commanded the British fleet destined for the Mediterranean, was sixty-nine years of age; but in the opinion of the most illustrious of his captains, Horatio Nelson, he still possessed the spirit and energy of a man of forty. Descended from a good family, he had had varied experiences. Serving as able seaman in the years 1741–3, and afterwards making his way from midshipman to the rank of vice-admiral (1787), he knew thoroughly all details of the service. Fortune had pressed hard on him, compelling him to serve under the unfortunate Graves at the Battle of Cape Henry in 1781, and under Rodney at the Battle of the Saints (April 12, 1782). On both occasions his daring and independent mind resented the conduct of the commander-in-chief, and he passed the following very severe criticism on the latter action:

> Surely there never was an instance before of a great fleet so completely beaten and routed, and *not pursued*....Had it been my lot to have commanded H.M.'s fleet on the 12th and have passed by so very clear and favourable an opportunity of raising the glory of my country, as I am grieved to say *was done*, I should have thought my head would have been justly required for such a glaring and shameful neglect.

Later on, he criticized Admiral Pigot for loitering along, and never exercising the fleet during a voyage of six weeks. Indeed he once admitted that he was "too open and honest-hearted to live in these times, and my mind often tells me I express my thoughts too freely; but I cannot help it[1]." On the one great occasion before 1793 when Hood was in command of a fleet, he displayed brilliant originality, viz. at Frigate Bay in St Christopher's (St Kitt's) when he challenged and tempted the French fleet out of its very advantageous berth and neatly slipped in to one that dominated it (January 1782). This brilliant nautical joke endeared

---

[1] *Letters of Sir S. Hood*, ed. by D. Hannay (N.R.S.), pp. 136, 145, 148.

Hood to every sailor; and in the judgment of his most famous successor he was the greatest seaman of that generation[1].

Hood had the defects of his qualities. He was apt to be censorious, and his impulsiveness often led him into exaggeration; but his warmheartedness and cheeriness won him the devotion of subordinates, and carried him through difficulties insuperable to mediocre or desponding natures. He was a great admiral because he was a keen, resolute and high-souled man. With any one of his former chiefs in command at Toulon, the place would have been very soon lost. On the other hand, his opinionated ways and dogmatic tone increased the difficulty of working with those impracticable allies, the Spaniards and French Royalists; while his full-blooded optimism led him, early in the defence, somewhat to understate the difficulties of that enterprise.

Hood's ardent spirit chafed at the long delays which deferred his departure from Spithead; but they were inevitable. Firstly, the supplies for the navy passed by Parliament on December 20, 1792, were for only 20,000 seamen and 5000 marines. On February 11, 1793, it granted supplies for 20,000 extra men, inclusive of 4000 marines; but of course these men were not forthcoming, still less efficient, during several months. Consequently (as has already appeared) the task of manning the fleets needed for the observation of Brest and Toulon was very great. The calls on the service were manifold. Besides guarding the coasts against armed bands of Jacobins, who, it was expected, would seek to stir up rebellion among our numerous malcontents, the navy had to convoy to Holland the forces supporting our Dutch allies, to watch the French ports, cope with privateers, and prepare to satisfy the demands of our Mediterranean Allies. Further, in February one of the French squadrons succeeded in getting away to the West Indies; and the imperious need of safeguarding our most valuable group of colonies led the British Cabinet at once to despatch a squadron in pursuit. This decision caused the first delay in the sailing of Hood's fleet. In an undated letter to Lord Grenville Pitt gave his judgment in favour of the colonial expedition, even though it should "retard sending twenty sail to the Mediterranean probably for about a fortnight beyond the time

---

[1] Nicolas, I, 378, 487.

they would have gone otherwise." The letter is of interest as showing both the large share taken by Pitt in determining the wider issues of the naval war and also the extreme difficulty of meeting promptly the varied needs of the British Empire at the sudden outbreak of hostilities[1].

As has already appeared, French activities at Toulon caused much alarm to our friends and Allies in the Mediterranean; and it is significant that only Sardinia (a belligerent then very hard pressed) formed a compact with us until it was known that Hood's fleet was on the way. The other Mediterranean States temporized until British policy in that quarter was clear. Spain did not join us until May 25, Naples until July 12, and Austria until August 30. In May–June 1793 those States might well hesitate. A person who left Toulon on May 19 reported that eight sail-of-the-line and nine smaller vessels were ready for sea; while in addition twelve sail and five frigates could weigh anchor by the end of June and several more in July[2]. Among these were five sail from Brest, viz. 'Commerce de Marseille' (120), 'Duguay Trouin' (74), 'Patriote' (74), 'Orion' (74), 'Thémistocle' (74): also from Rochefort the 74's, 'Apollon,' 'Entreprenant,' and 'Généreux.' Their arrival portended vigorous measures against the Spanish fleet then in the Mediterranean. Tilly, French *chargé d'affaires* at Genoa, wrote strongly urging Admiral Trogoff, commanding the French fleet at Toulon, to attack the Spaniards before the British arrived; but he refused, obviously owing to the inexperience of the French crews[3]. Nevertheless, the Spanish Carthagena fleet having, as we have seen, been crippled by pestilence, the Spanish army campaigning on the eastern Pyrenees was long exposed to a blow from the Toulon force; and not until mid-August, when Langara's fleet of nineteen sail arrived from Ferrol and Vigo, was Spain

---

[1] *Dropmore P.*, II, 403. The date is there given conjecturally as June–July. From the fact that Hood's first contingent sailed early in April, and the last on May 22, I date the letter March.

The Sardinian ambassador at London, Comte de Front, was always urging the despatch of Hood's fleet, but reported to his Government on May 17 that part cause of the delay was the British request to Spain to put her fleet under Hood's command, which she refused [Turin Archives]. Not until July 14 did the Channel Fleet under Lord Howe set sail to watch the Brest Fleet long assembling in Quiberon Bay.

[2] F.O. Sardinia, Trevor to Grenville, June 19, 1793 (enclosure).

[3] Lévy-Schneider, *Jean Bon St André*, p. 425.

able to assert herself in the Mediterranean. Affairs were also going badly for the Allies in Nice. There and along the Genoese Riviera the pressure of French warships told heavily against the Austro-Sardinian force defending the Corniche coast road. Trevor complained that the delay in Hood's arrival had enabled the French troops to fortify several positions along the coast east of Nice, thus rendering far more difficult the recovery of that city, and, indeed, imperilling the defence of North Italy. Trevor had pointed out Toulon as the proper objective of Hood's fleet and the Allied forces. But, as the months passed, that plan seemed to recede into the distance.

Hood was also being detained by the demands of British merchants for the protection of trade. In the Instructions issued to him in April–May this topic occupies a leading place (see Appendix A). The final "secret" Instructions of May 18 lay stress on the need of guarding "the Trade" and storeships as far as Gibraltar, then of fighting or blockading the Toulon fleet. Finally, in view of the negotiations then proceeding, my Lords direct him

to co-operate as far as circumstances may permit with the commanders of the fleets and armies of the Powers above mentioned in carrying into effect such measures as (in the interval of the final establishment of such concert) may suggest themselves on the spot to your Lordship and the commanders of the said fleets and armies, who will no doubt be particularly instructed to communicate with you as to the most effectual means of acting against the common enemy.

Hood is then charged to cultivate intimate relations with the Allies, to protect their coasts, to undertake further operations in pursuance of the concert to be established with them, or to be ready to "return to England with the Trade which you shall have assembled." These Instructions prove that the occupation of Toulon was as yet unimagined. As Lord Chatham stated in a later memorandum, the plan of the Admiralty was for Hood to collect the Trade and then "come home to refit, in case circumstances should have rendered it safe to have left the Mediterranean even for a short time[1]." Consequently, the action of the French Royalists at Toulon must be judged as one that was entirely unforeseen and therefore unprovided for.

[1] Chatham MSS.

The Instructions of May 18 to Hood also reflect the uncertainty of the whole situation. Our ancient ally, Portugal, could be counted on to do something; but, the attitude of Spain, Naples, Prussia and Austria being doubtful, some degree of caution was only natural; and it is noteworthy that, not until July 8, when the treaty with Naples was known to be nearly complete, did Henry Dundas draw up the Mediterranean programme which will be noticed later.

For the present the Admiralty ordered convoy work that should precede the hoped-for offensive against Toulon. Hood's fleet, therefore, sailed out in fractions. Rear-Admiral Gell in the 'St George' (98) and seven other craft set sail early in April with orders to convoy merchantmen to the Azores, and then steer for Gibraltar. Vice-Admiral Cosby in the 'Windsor Castle' (98) and with four other sail-of-the-line weighed anchor on April 15 with a large convoy to the coasts of Spain and Portugal, off which he was to cruise until May 15, afterwards proceeding to Gibraltar. Vice-Admiral Hotham in the 'Britannia' (100), with four more sail and two frigates, left Spithead on May 11 to cruise off Ushant, there to await a large convoy from the East Indies, and see it safe into the Channel, thenceforth waiting for Hood off the Lizard. The commander-in-chief on May 20 was ordered to proceed to sea in the 'Victory' (100) so soon as he could muster seven sail-of-the-line, then join Hotham, and assist him in seeing that convoy into safety, then to stretch into the Bay of Biscay, cut off any French squadron cruising there, and finally make for Gibraltar. He sailed on May 23[1] but the convoy was so late in appearing that the most ardent of his captains (who had preceded him by a few days) wrote "What we have been sent out for is best known to the Great Folks in London: to us, it appears, only to hum the nation and make tools (fools?) of us[2]." Such were the thoughts of Nelson in the 'Agamemnon' (64) while beating about off the Lizard. The delay equally annoyed Hood; for it retarded his arrival at Gibraltar by about a month[3], and seriously altered the situation in the Mediterranean to the disadvantage of the Allies.

When completed by the arrival of all the sections at Gibraltar

---

[1] See Log of 'Victory' in Appendix C.   [2] Nicolas, I, 306.
[3] Hood to Lord St Helens (at Madrid), June 14, 1793.

his fleet comprised, besides the flagships named above, the following 74's: 'Alcide' (R. Linzee), 'Bedford' (R. Man), 'Berwick' (Sir
John Collins), 'Captain' (S. Reeve), 'Colossus' (C. M. Pole),
'Courageux' (W. Waldegrave), 'Egmont' (A. Dickson), 'Fortitude' (W. Young), 'Illustrious' (T. L. Frederick), 'Leviathan'
(Lord H. S. Conway), 'Robust' (Hon. G. K. Elphinstone), 'Ter-
rible' (S. Lutwidge); and the 64's 'Agamemnon' (H. Nelson) and
'Ardent' (R. M. Sutton)[1]. The frigates and corvettes doing service
in the Mediterranean during August–December 1793 included
'l'Aigle' (J. N. Inglefield), 'Aimable' (Sir H. Burrard, Bt.), 'Amphi-
trite' (J. Dickinson, later A. Hunt[2]), 'Bulldog' (G. Hope), 'Castor'
(T. Troubridge), 'Iris' (G. Lumsdaine), 'Juno' (S. Hood), 'Leda'
(G. Campbell), 'Lowestoft' (W. Wolseley), 'Meleager' (C. Tyler),
'Mermaid' (J. Trigge), 'Nemesis' (J. Woodley), 'Romney' (50)
(Hon. W. Paget), 'Romulus' (Jn. Sutton), 'St Albans' (J. Vashon),
'Tartar' (A. Guyot), 'Tisiphone' (B. Martin), the smaller craft
'Alert,' 'Camel,' 'Speedy' and 'Vigilant,' along with the fireships
'Conflagration' and 'Vulcan'[3]. In November 'Bulldog' left the
Mediterranean; and the storeship 'Gorgon' (C. W. Paterson)
joined the flag, as did 'Inconstant' (A. Montgomery) and 'Dido'
(Sir C. Hamilton) in December and January 1794 respectively.

After provisioning and watering with the utmost promptitude
at Gibraltar[4], Hood sailed on June 28 with the Mediterranean
convoy, which parted company on the next day under escort of
'St Albans' and 'Bulldog.' Off Alicante, on July 8, he sighted
the Spanish fleet of Don Borja who informed him of the reasons
for returning to Carthagena. The captain of the Spanish frigate
added that it was no wonder they were sickly for they had been
sixty days at sea[5].

A singular episode which now occurred threw light on Hood's

---

[1] James (I, 72) includes 'Diadem' (64) (A. Sutherland), but she did not
reach Toulon till Nov. 19; also 'Intrepid' (64) from end of August, but she
did not leave Plymouth till early in 1794.

[2] *Letters of Sir T. Byam Martin*, I, 174.

[3] 'Castor' in September left the Mediterranean for home. 'Aigle,' 'Bulldog,' 'Juno,' 'Romney,' 'St Albans,' were occupied almost entirely with
convoying the trade, while most of the others were told off for convoying
troopships and victuallers.

[4] *Journals and Letters of Sir T. Byam Martin*, I, 177.

[5] Nicolas, I, 312.

plans for assuring the supremacy of the British flag in the Mediterranean. Before leaving Gibraltar, he summoned on board the 'Victory' Captains Lumsdaine of the 'Iris,' and Byam Martin of the 'Tisiphone,' and instructed the former as senior officer to proceed to Tunis with the 'Tisiphone' and the 'Mermaid.' At Tunis Byam Martin was to deliver to Consul Perkins Magra an important letter bearing on British policy at the Court of the Bey of Tunis. After performing this duty, he was to rejoin Lumsdaine, who, proceeding to Tripoli, would deliver to the Bey of that city presents loaded on a transport. The ostensible aim was to secure the friendship of the Beys of Tunis and Tripoli, in order to assure supplies of food to the British fleet, and bring about the overthrow of French influence on the African coast. Arriving near Tunis, the 'Tisiphone' chased a French corvette inshore under the guns of a battery, but did not attack her in neutral waters. Coasting along, Byam Martin sighted in Tunis harbour 'le Duquesne' (74) and three French frigates, and signalled their presence to his commodore. Lumsdaine stood in to verify the fact, and, in face of this great superiority of force, called off Martin and pursued his course to Tripoli, sending the 'Mermaid' to warn the admiral of the presence of the French squadron at Tunis, and the non-delivery of the letter.

Hood took the news very ill, and declared his intention of trying both Lumsdaine and Byam Martin by court martial for disobedience to orders. In due course Martin rejoined the flag and pointed out that he had acted according to the directions of his senior officer, Lumsdaine. But during the interview Hood revealed the motive which had prompted the expedition to Tunis in spite of the presence of the French squadron.

I had fully calculated [so he said to Martin] that the French admiral would, in the rashness of their republican feelings, have captured the *Tisiphone*—at any rate it was my plan to put the temptation in his way; and if the bait had taken, I was prepared at once to make a general sweep of the French ships of war out of every neutral port.

Eventually Lumsdaine was tried by court martial at Toulon on board H.M.S. 'Britannia,' and honourably acquitted. Naturally enough Byam Martin was hurt at figuring as the cat's paw in

Hood's masterful game; but his account seems trustworthy, and it testifies to the admiral's hatred of the French and his resolve to use any means whatsoever for sweeping their ships out of the Mediterranean, even at the cost of Byam Martin's ship and crew, and despite the risk of widely scattering the British fleet in the attempt[1].

Meanwhile, contrary winds and calms delayed the British fleet on its voyage towards Toulon; so that not until July 16 did it sight Cape Cicié, to the south of that city. A little earlier Hood had despatched Captain Inglefield in 'l'Aigle' (36) with a letter for Trevor at Turin. On July 29, in port at Genoa, that frigate was insulted and molested by a French frigate, 'Modeste,' and two tartans, with results that will duly appear[2]. Even apart from this episode, the suspicious conduct of the Genoese Republic called for the presence of several of Hood's ships to observe that port, as also Spezzia, in order to stop the supplies of corn destined for the French armies.

Hood's letter to Trevor was destined to open up relations with that envoy and with a British officer, Lord Mulgrave, who was expected at Turin[3]. Before leaving London, Mulgrave had received very important "Instructions," signed on July 8 by Henry Dundas, one of the Secretaries of State. Proofs are not wanting that they were approved by Pitt and Grenville[4]. But their author was the bold, acquisitive laird, who practically governed British India, controlled the finance of the navy, dabbled in strategy, and kept close to heel the expectant squad of thirty-five Scottish members of Parliament. Hard-working, adroit and ambitious, Dundas, next to Pitt, was the most powerful man at Westminster. He possessed far more imagination than the cold and cautious Foreign Minister, Lord Grenville, and probably his Mediterranean policy, now to be noticed, as also his strenuous advocacy of the Egyptian expedition of 1801, arose from his anxiety respecting

---

[1] *Journals and Letters of Sir T. Byam Martin*, I, 188, 349–52.

[2] James (I, p. 72) wrongly dates Hood's arrival off Toulon as in the middle of August. He also omits to notice the action of 'Modeste' at Genoa.

[3] Henry Phipps, first Earl of Mulgrave (1755–1831) was colonel of the 31st Regiment. The *Dict. of National Biography* states that he chanced to be a visitor on Hood's ship; but, as is shown above, he came on an important mission.

[4] *Dropmore P.*, II, 392, 399, 407–8, 419.

our communications with India, which must be endangered by French control of that sea.

Dundas now instructed Lord Mulgrave to proceed to Turin with the aim of concerting measures with that Court and the Habsburg Power, for the recovery of Savoy and Nice. But this was not all. Dundas declared that, "if sufficient military force can be collected, it might be beneficially directed, in co-operation with the fleet, to the capture of Toulon, Marseilles and Corsica," in that autumn or early in 1794. To this end Austria must be induced to increase her corps of 8000 men already serving with the Sardinians by ten or twelve thousand troops now in her Milanese province. Further, by a treaty about to be concluded with the King of Naples and Sicily, that monarch would assist Great Britain in the Mediterranean with 6000 troops, four sail-of-the-line and eight smaller vessels. Finally, German or Swiss contingents might be hoped for, which would raise the total of troops to 40,000, or possibly to 50,000 men. Mulgrave was to set these projects in good train, inspecting also the contingents as they arrived, and concerting measures with Hood and the British ministers in Italy[1].

The recovery of Nice for Sardinia, the siege of Toulon by an Austro-Sardinian force and a British fleet, the blockade and capture of Marseilles, finally the driving of the French from Corsica—such was the programme. It would be carried out almost solely by Allied troops, for England had very few to spare. Her scanty numbers went part to Flanders, some to the West Indies, while others were needed to repress malcontents at home. Nevertheless, Dundas's fertile imagination pictured an easy triumph over France. Seven weeks later he penned a forecast of the events of 1794. The French armies having been overthrown in the north, Toulon and Brest were to be besieged by the Allied fleet and armies, and then—"this country, having captured the French West India Islands and destroyed their existing fleet, may long rest in quiet."

---

[1] H.O. Mil. Med. 1793. The efforts to bring Switzerland into the First Coalition failed. See *Dropmore P.*, II, 457, 467. Grenville wrote to Dundas on August 6 or 7: "The two obvious means of employing them [the Neapolitan forces at our disposal] are either to co-operate in the recovery of Nice &c., or to make a separate expedition to relieve Corsica, while Lord Hood keeps the French fleet at bay" (*Dropmore P.*, II, 411).

Quitting the sphere of vinous speculations, we return to Lord Hood. After a brush of his light craft and the 'Illustrious' with two French frigates on the night of July 15 (which Nelson thought very unsatisfactory), the fleet rounded up a French corvette, 'l'Eclair' (22). On July 19, after sighting Cape Cicié, south of Toulon, Hood decided to send Lieutenant Cooke of the 'Victory' with a flag of truce to the governor of Toulon, with a proposal for an exchange of prisoners as against the crew of 'l'Eclair'[1]. The real motive was to gain information as to the strength of the French fleet. There is no reason to suppose that Hood had any knowledge of the civil strifes in France. Certainly he cannot have heard of the victory of the moderates over the Jacobins of Toulon city on July 13. There is nothing to support the statements of French historians (especially Chevalier[2]), who assert that Hood came charged with a mission to treat with the Toulonese for the restoration of monarchy. Still less is there any ground for the insinuation of Jomini that Hood now proceeded to act up to his rôle of a born intriguer[3]. The approach of Cooke's boat near to the French fleet elicited a signal proof of the still fervid Republicanism of the crews. He was sharply ordered to lower his white flag and hoist the tricolour in deference to national sentiment. He was also forbidden to go beyond the topic of the exchange of prisoners. Finally, however, Governor Doumet returned answer that the prisoners of the Allied nations were distant a three days' journey, but could be exchanged if desired. The reception accorded to Cooke is significant; for a week had elapsed since the moderates of Toulon maintained that they were the true Republicans[4]. Indeed, at Toulon, as at Marseilles and Lyons, nothing but the terrorism of the extremists brought the moderates to adopt Royalism. At this time Cooke met with little encouragement, and he merely brought back a few British prisoners together with news that the French had sixteen sail-of-the-line in the outer road and were fitting out five in the harbour. A Danish merchant captain, however, who set sail from Toulon on July 26, reported that, when Cooke's brig appeared

---

[1] E. Cooke was son of Col. Cooke of Harefield (not of Capt. James Cook as Cottin states p. 69). He died of wounds received in the capture of the 'Forte' in 1799.

[2] Chevalier, p. 73.   [3] Jomini, I, 217.   [4] Pons, pp. 16–25.

off Toulon, "many people were for the English and forty were taken up, and the day after about the same number were taken up and put in prison[1]."

A severe northerly gale of three days' duration now fell on Hood's fleet. It carried away the mainmast of the 'Robust,' and topmasts of three other ships, beside breaking the bowsprit and tophamper of the 'Berwick' (a bad sailor) and driving her from the fleet. She had to run to Gibraltar, and the frigate 'Meleager' to Port Mahon, for repairs[2]. Hood's fleet was badly scattered; but the Toulon fleet, though numbering sixteen sail in good trim, against his eighteen damaged and scattered ships, did not come out to fight.

Meanwhile the barbarities of Barras and Fréron, the *Représentants en mission* to Provence, drove the Provençaux further towards Royalism, a tendency which was far more marked in Toulon itself than on the fleet in the harbour. There were sharp divisions on the ships, the crews from the Atlantic ports declaring for the Red Republic, while those of the Toulon ships (except St Julien's ship 'Le Commerce de Bordeaux') went with the townsfolk. The leading men in Toulon favoured either a moderate Republic or a monarchy of the type established by the constitution of 1791. As for the populace, the conversion was hastened by Jacobinical atrocities and by the advance towards Marseilles of General Carteaux with a Jacobin column detached from the army of the Alps. Further south Generals La Barre and Lapoye began to advance from the County of Nice westwards on Toulon. The danger served to turn the thoughts of both towns towards the British fleet.

Marseilles was the first to send overtures to Hood. Threatened by the approach of Carteaux, that city saw its supplies from the interior in danger, while the British fleet cut off the convoys of corn from Genoa, Leghorn, and Tunis. Accordingly, on August 17, the Marseillais despatched to Toulon two deputies to propose terms of alliance. As the General Committee at Toulon hesitated, Marseilles on the 21st despatched two envoys direct to the British admiral, ostensibly in order to procure a permit for the free

---

[1] F.O. Sardinia, 12, Trevor to Grenville, July 30.
[2] *Recollections of J. A. Gardiner*, p. 127.

passage of eight corn ships blockaded in Genoa or Leghorn, but in reality in order to come to terms with Hood. He in the 'Victory' and with a considerable part of his fleet was then cruising off the Hières Islands, inside which there was a good roadstead, about fifteen miles south-east of Toulon. The Marseilles envoys, representing their Department, came charged with full powers to treat for peace. On their declaring themselves in favour of monarchy, the admiral drew up and sent ashore a Proclamation and Preliminary Declaration urging the restoration of monarchy as the only means of assuaging misrule, and offering peace and protection from Great Britain and her allies. On the 24th or early on the 25th there arrived Commissioners from Toulon whom those from Marseilles had expected to find aboard. These went further and offered to deliver to Hood the harbour and forts of Toulon. To this he at first demurred, on the ground of the insufficiency of his military force and the decided opposition of a large part of the French fleet. But he resolved to anchor in Hières Bay, where the batteries had been secured, and be ready thence to offer what help he could. Indeed, Hood was in no very favourable position. On the 22nd he had written to the commander of the Spanish fleet, now off Roussillon, stating that want of water would compel the British fleet to go to port by the 31st, and requesting him to come to observe Toulon. As, however, Hood then heard that that fleet could not leave its station, he wrote again urging the despatch of at least a squadron, with as many Spanish troops as possible. He also wrote to Naples and Turin begging those Courts to send military succour. His hopeful nature finds expression in the forecast—"Had I 5000 or 6000 good troops with me, the war would soon be at an end[1]." He did not know that on that very day the Royalist defence at Marseilles miserably collapsed, the city being occupied and pillaged by the hordes of Carteaux. In point of fact, Hood arrived a fortnight too late to rescue the Royalist cause in Provence.

It is clear, then, that Hood was surprised by the offers from Marseilles and Toulon, and at first hesitated to accept because

---

[1] Adm. Med. 1793, Hood to P. Stephens, Aug. 25 (see Appendix E). The second sentence is incorrectly quoted by Cottin, p. 413; he also omits the P.S. For the bad results of Hood's optimism, see Fortescue, IV (Pt. I), p. 138.

he had no effective means of accepting them. The initiative came entirely from the shore, not from him. It is probable that his blockade had increased the discomfort of the Provençaux, but clearly the malcontents had exaggerated the shortage of food. Hatred of the Terrorist rule, and a resolve to cast it off by the help of the British and Spanish fleets—these were the motives prompting their action. Alliance with Britain and Spain, not surrender to them, such was the programme; and Hood perfectly understood it. The fact must be insisted on because certain officials at home gave out that Toulon surrendered to Hood, and that therefore he had a right to do what he would with the French fleet and stores[1]. The reverse was the case. So long as Toulon held out on behalf of the French monarchy, it was held in trust; and Hood scorned the disgraceful thought of burning the French ships and then leaving the Toulonese to their fate.

The all-important fact that Toulon was held in trust was made clear in Hood's Declaration and Proclamation of August 23. Those documents, having been published in the *Annual Register* for 1793, the *Naval Chronicle* for 1799, and in M. Cottin's *Toulon et les Anglais*, may be very briefly summarized here. In the Declaration he states that if the *fleur de lys* be hoisted at Toulon and Marseilles, the warships disarmed and the harbours and forts placed in his power, he will give the Provençaux all the aid that his fleet can procure, promising further to respect life and property; and when peace is made (*i.e.* with the restored monarchy) the French ships and munitions will be restored. The Proclamation recounts in rhetorical style the miseries of Jacobin rule and offers loyally and generously to assist in re-establishing the monarchy.

On the 25th, as we have seen, the Jacobin column from the army of the Alps, under Carteaux, overcame the Royalists of Marseilles. Consequently the Allies were too late to assist in the defence of that important city, the loss of which was a serious blow to the monarchist movement in southern France. Thanks, however, to the enterprise of Lieut. Cooke, who again made his way to shore, Toulon on that same day decided to accede to Hood's terms. The General Committee of the Sections replied that

---

[1] *E.g.* Lord Chatham in an undated mem. on the Toulon affair (Chatham MSS. 364) wrote: "After Toulon capitulated...."

they would provisionally place the citadel and forts at his disposal but trusted that the garrisons would consist equally of French and British, the command however devolving upon the latter[1]. The agreement therefore was complete, though the stipulation as to equal French and British forces in the citadel and forts was destined to cause friction.

Nevertheless, a considerable part of the population and a majority of the Toulon fleet strongly opposed this decision. Of the seventeen French sail-of-the-line then anchored in the outer road, eleven were for the Republic; and it is probable that of the grand total, sixteen opposed the decision of the townsfolk. On the 25th the Jacobinical crews succeeded in deposing the now Royalist Admiral Trogoff and installed in command Rear-Admiral St Julien, "a man of turbulent mind," as Hood terms him. They also seized the forts of Éguillette and Balaguier on the west of the entrance, and the batteries on the Cepet Peninsula. The seventeen ships were moored in a crescent between those positions, but do not seem to have planned a fight with Hood's squadron (then only twelve sail strong) as Nelson expected[2]. In fact, the Republican crews were themselves divided, none of the Provençaux officers and seamen being desirous of seeing Toulon fall into the hands of the Jacobin forces now advancing upon it. Moreover, Fort La Malgue and the Great Tower were preparing to fire red-hot shot upon the Jacobinical ships. Parleys therefore took place on August 25 and 26 with the Royalists, who pointed out that Toulon had but five days' provisions and therefore it was necessary to come to terms with the British fleet. Loud protests against the shame of letting in the enemy arose from the Jacobins, especially those from the western ports, while the Provençaux firmly stood out for alliance with the foreigner rather than surrender all that they held dear to the Terrorists. Finally an understanding was reached, that the crews of the western ports should be sent to their homes under a safe conduct[3]. Probably

---

[1] *Ann. Reg.* (1793), p. 172; *Naval Chronicle* (1799), Pt. II, p. 104. The document, signed by twenty-five citizens, is not printed by Cottin.

[2] Nicolas, I, 324.

[3] Pons (p. 82) states that the French crews were much influenced by the arrival of Lieut. Cooke from the 'Victory' with the offer that Hood would pay them in silver.

the victory of the moderates on board the French ships was assisted by the return on the 27th of Vice-Admiral Cosby's squadron from Genoa, comprising the 'Windsor Castle' (98), and 'Terrible' and 'Bedford' (74's), with the 'Vulcan' fireship. On that day also Royalist fugitives from Marseilles poured into Toulon, thereby increasing the number of mouths to feed and filling the city with tales of the scenes of horror from which they had escaped. Clearly Toulon must either abase herself before the Terrorists or confide her fortunes to Admiral Hood. She chose the latter course. The French fleet seemed inclined to resist; but at 10 a.m. the frigate 'Perle' hoisted the flag of the commander-in-chief Trogoff, and ordered the fleet to retire into the inner harbour. Seven Toulonese ships obeyed. Thereupon St Julien hauled down his flag and Fort La Malgue signalled to Hood to approach. The Jacobinical crews gave up all thought of resistance and many of their seamen escaped to shore in boats or by swimming, and sought to reach Marseilles. St Julien, failing in his attempt, gave himself up to Hood, who ultimately handed him on to the Spaniards.

Perhaps the final collapse of the Jacobin defence was hastened by the sight in the offing of the Spanish fleet under Admiral Langara, including seventeen sail-of-the-line[1]. Early on the 28th Hood ordered all the troops on board his fleet to proceed to the 'Robust' with a view to a landing under the command of her captain, the Honble. Keith Elphinstone. At 7.30 a.m. the following ships stood in towards the outer road—'Egmont,' 'Robust,' 'Colossus,' 'Courageux,' and the frigates 'Meleager' and 'Tartar'; and at 11.30 the troops landed without opposition, followed by seamen (some 1500 in all) to help man the forts[2]. The great Fort La Malgue was delivered up by the Royalist garrison, and the other forts and the city itself were occupied. The rest of the British ships, soon followed by the Spaniards, anchored in the outer road whence the Frenchmen had withdrawn. The arrival of the Spaniards and the landing of about 1000 of their men were opportune, but there is no reason for thinking that it materially altered the situation on August 28. All the arrangements were

---

[1] Duro, *op. cit.*, VIII, p. 33.
[2] Log of 'Princess Royal' (Capt. Purvis). See Appendix C.

with Hood, the Spaniards becoming accessories after the negotiation and occupation were completed[1].

The responsibility for the occupation of Toulon and the terms on which it was effected rested entirely with Hood. The whole affair bespeaks his hopeful and determined character. Perhaps his offers of help to the Royalists were excessive in view of the fact that Naples could not send effective aid and Spain was lukewarm in the common cause. Such at least was the opinion of the oldest and most experienced of European statesmen. After the arrival at Vienna of news of a reverse at Toulon the former Chancellor of Austria, Prince Kaunitz, expressed his astonishment at the lightheartedness of Hood in accepting from the Toulonese conditions that were *peu profitables*, and in occupying the place with means insufficient to defend it[2].

"What an event this has been for Lord Hood" (so wrote Nelson to his wife): "...that the strongest place in Europe, and 22 sail-of-the-line should be given up without firing a shot. It is not to be credited." Nelson did not witness the completion of this memorable event. No sooner was the negotiation concluded than he was despatched with urgent requests for troops from the Courts of Turin and Naples; for here was the weak side of the enterprise as the young captain had already surmised. 'It seems of no use" (he wrote on August 20, when off Toulon) "to send a great Fleet here without troops to act with them[3]." Pitt having in the spring of 1792 cut down the army to 17,000 men, very few could now be spared for the Mediterranean. The intention had been that the British fleet should protect the Trade, help Sardinia, and then return with the Mediterranean convoy. But now we were allied to Austria, Sardinia, Spain and Naples, and the French Royalists had confided to us the defence of Toulon. The question was—Would these Powers do their utmost to make good use of this opportunity?

The immediate results of the occupation of Toulon by the British and Spanish fleets were very great. That event weakened the French Atlantic fleet by eight sail-of-the-line and paralysed

[1] "Troops landed and occupied Grand Work near Toulon: the Spanish Fleet in the offing, 7 or 8 miles" (Captain's Log of 'Alcide').

[2] Marquis de Breme to the King, Oct. 3 (Turin Archives).

[3] Nicolas, I, 324. Nelson's view, that Toulon surrendered, was incorrect.

the naval power of the French Republicans in the Mediterranean, turning against them the blow they were preparing against the coasts of Spain and Naples. Further, by cutting off the food that had gone by sea from Genoa and Leghorn to the Republican forces in the Maritime Alps, Hood greatly embarrassed them and brought about a situation from which the Austro-Sardinian army ought to have profited. His success also established a powerful centre of Royalist influence, which, with due backing, might effectively have helped Lyons and other towns and districts opposed to the new Parisian despotism. The tidings from Toulon caused a profound sensation at Paris, imperilling for a few days the existence of the Committee of Public Safety, the mainspring of the Jacobin machine.

CHAPTER III

THE ALLIES AND TOULON

WARLIKE enterprises often suffer from the easy success with which fortune favours the first efforts; and this truth is especially applicable to the Allied occupation of Toulon. Crowning the successes of the Allies and the Vendéans in the summer of 1793, it promised, as Hood wrote, soon to end the war. To an ordinary government it would have been fatal; on the national pride of the newly emancipated French it acted merely as a spur to further and more furious effort. After the first feelings of consternation wore off a spirit of defiance permeated the capital and France at large. "We will conquer without Toulon," cried Robespierre[1]. Thanks to the wonderful energy of the Committee, which was now enforcing the new law of conscription, the nation rallied to its side. France for the time became Jacobinical in order to expel the foreign invaders and crush domestic treason. She had, what the Allies lacked, unity of purpose and abundance of men.

Moreover, the defence of Toulon was far more difficult than appeared on the surface. A glance at the plan shows that the city and the inner harbour are dominated by several heights, the loss of any of which must compromise the defence. Of these the most prominent was Mt Faron, some 1700 feet high, having a precipitous northern face, scaleable only at *le Pas de la Masque*. The fortifications had been designed for defence against an invader coming from Italy; and on that eastern side they were of great strength. They centred in Fort La Malgue, mounting 148 guns, which dominated the outer roadstead and the eastern approaches to the city. The forts, St Catherine, Artigues and Faron (the last on an eastern spur of the mountain) completed these works. On the west, however, the only important defences were the Pomets Fort (faulty both in position and design) and Malbousquet Fort. The latter, though it commanded the course of a brook coming down from the north, was of no great strength,

---

[1] *Histoire parlementaire*, XXIX, p. 199. See too *Dropmore P.*, II, 460.

and needed outworks to render it tenable. Unfortunately, the Allies had at hand no trustworthy engineer officers who could scientifically strengthen these defences; consequently the new works were defective. The most considerable were outworks to Malbousquet and behind it supporting batteries on the Missiessi hillocks. The Allies also put up what Thaon de Revel calls a kind of fort at St Antoine and Little St Antoine; and they erected a redoubt at La Croix de Faron, the highest point of the mountain, and a battery at Cape Brun to protect the fleet in the outer roadstead. No guns were placed in St Antoine until Sept. 23.

Later on, as we shall see, they constructed an intrenched position on La Grasse heights, above the Balaguier and Éguillette coast batteries. They also protected the Cepet Peninsula by Les Sablettes battery commanding the isthmus. There was a capital defect in these defences, namely, that the loss of any one of them compromised the safety either of the town or of the fleet. Experience soon showed another defect, viz. that the shallowness of the western end of the inner harbour prevented Hood's heavy ships from lying close in so as to bring their big guns to bear effectively on the Republican batteries soon to be erected near the coast. Frigates, corvettes and gun-vessels were therefore urgently needed; and of these neither Hood nor Langara had a sufficient supply. True, there were several in Toulon[1]; but, for some reason hard to explain, they were not utilized very effectively[2]. A less obvious but even more serious difficulty for Hood was the length of time taken in communicating with his Government. On the average a despatch took about three weeks to reach London[3], while the besiegers got through news to Paris in about four days. Consequently time and space worked potently for the Republicans, who had the further advantage of depending only on themselves, while Hood depended largely on difficult and untrustworthy allies. The sequel will show the heavy drag of a cumbrous loose-limbed Coalition, and the immense advantage of swiftly acting central control. Carnot, the personification of

[1] See *Naval Chron.* (1797), p. 298.
[2] Probably Hood and Langara distrusted the crews of the French frigates, but they afterwards used the prize 'l'Aurore' and other small craft.
[3] Grenville heard the news of Hood's entry into Toulon on Sept. 13.

energy, worked along an arc; the Allies straggled and struggled round the circumference of a circle.

From the configuration and relief of the land about Toulon it followed that the presence of the Allied fleets extended the area which had to be defended. Further, it was impossible for forty sail-of-the-line to lie conveniently in the two roadsteads, the outer of which is too much exposed to Levanters to afford a safe anchorage[1]. Yet, in default of troops, Hood and Langara needed the crews of the ships; and on these at first fell the chief burdens of the defence, extra drafts being sent on shore as occasion demanded.

They saved the situation on August 31. Carteaux, who commanded the Republican forces now triumphant at Marseilles (or more probably his advisers), had correctly gauged the weakness of the defence at Toulon. Warned, doubtless by bands of Republican sailors who were straggling on towards Marseilles, he saw the immense advantage of capturing the village of la Seyne. There he hoped to come into touch with some of the French crews, who might be induced to avenge the insult to the French tricolour. His outposts now held the outskirts of the village of Ollioules; and at 2 a.m. of August 30 he sent off a despatch to warn Colonel Mouret, holding that important position, that he would speedily receive reinforcements in men and guns, and must thereupon advance and seize first la Seyne, second the height commanding the powder magazine of Milau on the shore to the south of Fort Malbousquet. La Seyne he declared to be held only by a few ragamuffins. He added that the defenders could not possibly hold all the forts, their troops being very indifferent; and he encouraged Mouret by the partly false statement that General La Barre with 8000 men and fourteen guns from the French "Army of Italy" had come up and taken, not only the village of la Valette, northeast of Toulon, but also Forts Artigues and St Catherine, the keys of its eastern defences. He therefore expected soon to cut in pieces the Toulonese "as well as the English and Spanish scoundrels[2]." The letter shows how quickly Carteaux and his advisers discerned the weak points of the Allied defence, and how

[1] Brenton, I, 197.
Adm. Med. (1793); Naval Chron. (1799), pp. 110–12.

confident they were of crushing it forthwith. On the whole the optimism of Carteaux was not ill founded. From the first he discerned in la Seyne an important point for attack; and his discernment should have screened him from the unrelieved ridicule which Bonaparte and all subsequent writers poured upon him. If La Barre had been in a position to help him by an attack from the east, Toulon must have fallen.

Hood's fleet had on board only some 1200 troops[1]. By the afternoon of August 29 the chief forts and the city were in their hands. Lieut. Cooke commanded the sailors, charged to occupy the forts and the city, while the command of the British troops on shore devolved for the present on Captain Elphinstone, R.N., whose firm and judicious character, fortified by experience on land under Sir Henry Clinton at the siege of Charleston (1780), soon proved to be of high value. In view of Nelson's strong prejudice against Elphinstone after he became Admiral Lord Keith, we may note that in October 1793 he pronounced him a good officer and gallant man[2]. The Spanish troops, which were landed on the 29th and 30th, were placed under the command of Rear-Admiral Gravina, whose courage and tact won general admiration.

Scarcely were the forts and walls in the hands of the Allies when Elphinstone received urgent requests from the Toulonese Committee of War and Safety to defend the place from the threatened attack of Carteaux. The Republican vanguard, under Mouret, some 600 strong, on August 30 occupied Ollioules and Senary, wounding several peasants at both places. On the afternoon of the 31st they were throwing out companies on their left to seize a height nearer Toulon when Elphinstone's force came on the scene. Quickly assembling 300 British troops and as many Spaniards from the eastern forts, he requested the Toulon Committee to support him with some of their best troops and six cannon. This succour was not forthcoming, but Hood, on hearing the news, at once sent ashore 400 seamen to garrison the posts

---

[1] By Sept. 14 the total of officers, N.C.O.'s and privates was 1626 (of which 365 were on Hood's frigates). The 'Berwick' did not land her troops at Toulon until early in October (H.O. Mil. Med., Mulgrave to Dundas, Sept. 15, 1793). The 29th regiment went on board Hood's fleet as marines (*Dropmore P.*, II, 424). The British troops included not a single artillery-man (see Mulgrave's letter in Appendix F).

[2] Nicolas, I, 333.

thus denuded of troops; and we may here note that at every sortie the fleet acted as feeder to the forces ashore. Without waiting for the French reinforcement, Elphinstone pushed on westwards, and, arriving at the scene of action, detached a part of the 11th regiment under Captains Haddon and Wemys to save the height, and also to occupy a ridge farther west. Thus flanking the advance of his main body on the lower ground, he proceeded to reconnoitre Ollioules. He found the enemy strongly posted, but an advance equally skilful and dashing drove them out of the village. Then, at nightfall, his ammunition being nearly exhausted, and the guides having fled, Elphinstone judged it dangerous to remain in an unknown position. He therefore retired on Toulon and on the way met the Royalist troops and cannon which should have supported him in the afternoon. In this brilliant little affair the British had thirteen men wounded; the Spaniards three killed and two wounded. On September 1 Hood appointed Elphinstone to command the British troops in the eastern forts, Rear-Admiral Goodall Governor of Toulon, and Rear-Admiral Gravina "Commandant of the Troops."

Considering all the circumstances, the success of the Allies at Ollioules was highly creditable; and, had effective help been forthcoming from the Toulon National Guard, that important position might have been strongly held and formed the basis for offensive operations. As it was, that post was occupied by a small Spanish garrison and proved to be a source of anxiety in the defensive warfare to which the Allies were condemned by the paucity of their trustworthy troops. Optimism found expression in the phrase of Hood's report to the Admiralty—"am very confident we can hold what we have got against a thousand Carteaux." His confidence was excessive seeing that to the east of Toulon the Republicans held villages up to within two miles of the town. In any case, the expression of that confidence was unwise as it tended to increase the optimism of officials at home. To do them justice, they made praiseworthy efforts. On September 14 Grenville stated that 5000 men would sail in about a fortnight, and other plans were afoot for augmenting gradually the forces at Toulon, some of those destined for co-operation with the army of Devins being diverted thither. Therefore the only fear was just for the present while Hood's force was small[1]. Grenville also urged the Sardinian ambassador, Count de Front, that Devins must make all possible efforts to recapture Nice and then press on to Toulon, or, preferably, embark some of his troops to reinforce that garrison[2]. In view of these facts it is clear that at first the British Government put forth considerable efforts for the Toulon enterprise. Langara also did his utmost. In a letter begging for succour from the Spanish army in Roussillon, he declared that events at Toulon and in Provence might be so decisive as to put an end to the war on the most honourable terms. General Ricardos, commanding that army, was however so hard pressed by the French that he despatched to Toulon only the refuse of his army[3].

The difficulties of the situation at Toulon were forcibly set forth in a letter written on September 14 by a British officer to Lord St Helens, British ambassador at Madrid. Their scanty forces were quite inadequate for defence of the town and forts, but hitherto they were little troubled by Carteaux, whose force of 5000 men, consisting largely of peasants forced into the ranks, straggled over from one to three leagues west of the town. La Barre's army on the east was more numerous but equally inactive. We cannot (he continued) attack either force owing to the un-trustworthiness of the Toulonese, and the hostility of some 6000 sailors of their fleet; for we have on shore only 1171 British and 3166 Spaniards, with 400 British and 300 Spanish seamen, besides others landed in case of alarm. When strong enough, we shall enrol "about 6000 of the large armed mob which we have within the walls, and the remainder will be disarmed, and those most suspected sent away." The town is within cannon shot of the spurs of Mt Faron, and there are many houses outside of the walls, which we dare not yet clear away. "We have three French engineers said to be skilful and apparently zealous; but, tho' the workmen are paid in money, it is impossible to carry on the works fast, and it is extremely difficult to procure the necessary stores

---

[1] F.O. Sardinia, Grenville to Trevor, Sept. 14.

[2] De Front to Count Hauteville, Sept. 17 (Turin Archives). Trevor at first disbelieved in success opposite Nice and urged the sending of Sardinian troops to Toulon, but on October 3 advocated the Nice offensive because things were easy at Toulon (F.O. Sardinia, 12, Trevor to Grenville, Sept. 14, Oct. 3).

[3] *Elliot, Life*, II, 191.

from the arsenal, they being in the keeping of the town committees, whose members are all ignorant and for the most part ill disposed." The five three-deckers and 'Robust' are the only British ships present, also several Spaniards. They have springs on their cables so as to be able to haul round and annoy the enemy on shore[1].

Difficulties soon arose as to the command of the troops. Co-operation with the Spaniards was always a delicate affair; but Hood had taken care to humour Admiral Langara by at once paying him a ceremonial visit and then by proceeding with him to interview the civic authorities at Toulon, to whom he significantly stated "We two are only one." Differences, however, soon arose on the topic just mentioned. On August 31 or September 1 Hood requested Rear-Admiral Gravina to be commandant of the troops on shore, and he seems not to have attached any reservations or conditions to this request[2]. The appointment was of an informal character, and it was natural and proper seeing that the Spanish and French Royalist troops at that time outnumbered the British. The situation altered later on when the Sardinian and Neapolitan contingents arrived, for they were subsidized by Great Britain; and it was unreasonable that the British and subsidized contingents, forming the majority of the whole force, should be commanded by a Spaniard. Further (as will be seen by the letter of the King of Naples printed in Appendix E), that monarch placed the whole of the Neapolitan troops entirely at Hood's disposal, and the Neapolitan minister, General Acton, added that they were not to act under the orders of any other Power. So long as Rear-Admiral Gravina held that command on shore no difficulties arose. Indeed, after the arrival of Lord Mulgrave (soon to be noticed) Gravina seems voluntarily to have limited his command to the Spanish troops[3].

The need of sending away the disaffected French sailors, some 5000 in number, soon became acute. Indeed, so great was the danger that Hood wrote to the Admiralty on September 13, "I am more afraid of an enemy within than without." He therefore

[1] F.O. Spain, 28, Anon. to St Helens, Sept. 14, enclosed in his of Sept. 25 to Grenville.
[2] Hood to the Admiralty, Sept. 1, 1793. See Appendix E.
[3] *London Gazette*, Oct. 5, 1793.

used all possible expedition in despatching the malcontents on the least serviceable of the French 74's, 'Apollon,' 'Entreprenant,' 'Orion' and 'Patriote.' These he disarmed, leaving on board only two small guns for signalling purposes; and on September 15 they set sail with safe conducts for the Biscay ports. The Spanish Government complained of the loss of four French sail-of-the-line; but they were old and inefficient ships, of little or no value in war, and not worth overhauling. Further, Hood had promised to send these men away, and to retain them at Toulon for the sake of four nearly rotten ships would have been a strange act of economy, likely to lead to the betrayal of the whole place to the Jacobins[1]. The departure of the "refractory" seamen did not end the anxieties of Hood concerning his French allies. He had closely to watch certain crews and battalions, whose fidelity depended on punctual payments in silver. The expenses of the defence being very heavy, he found it necessary to despatch the frigate 'Romulus' to Naples to open a fund for £20,000. In part this was needed for the equipment of a battalion formed from among the best French troops of the line in Toulon. Though under French discipline and commanded by officers appointed directly by the Comte de Provence, it was to be supported by British money and be at the disposal of the British Government. The officers of the new battalion were appointed from among those already in Toulon, whose record was satisfactory. As formed on October 12, it comprised only 395 officers and men. Three or four companies of *chasseurs* were also raised; but the Allies left unsolved the problem of dealing with the large mass of half-disciplined French soldiers and National Guards, whose numbers have been reckoned as high as 17,000 or 18,000[2]. Unfortunately Hood found it impossible to send any of them away, and their presence seriously clogged the defence.

Meanwhile, on September 7, to Hood's great relief, Lord Mulgrave arrived from Turin[3]. That officer, now Colonel of the

---

[1] Jomini (IV, 215) absurdly states that the four ships were sent off to Rochefort and Brest, "afin d'y donner accès aux coalisés par une trame semblable."

[2] Cottin, p. 146.

[3] Henry Phipps, first Earl of Mulgrave and Viscount Normanby (1755–1831). As has been noticed on p. 16, he came on a mission, and was not a visitor on Hood's ship.

31st regiment, had seen service during the American War and then in the West Indies. Being deputed by the Government to proceed to Turin and develop its Mediterranean policy, he now made his way to Toulon. Hood requested that Mulgrave should hold locally the rank of Brigadier-General. But on September 26 Dundas wrote to Major-General O'Hara, then at Gibraltar, appointing him Governor of Toulon in place of Rear-Admiral Goodall. The Pitt Administration (he wrote) resolved to hold the city, "with a view to ulterior offensive operations," for which purpose it proposed to send 5000 Hessians immediately, also a large part of the garrison at Gibraltar, three regiments of cavalry from Ireland, about 1000 sabres strong, and the flank companies of foot regiments in Ireland amounting to 2000 men. Also Austria was to be urged to despatch forthwith 5000 troops then in the Milanese.

The proposal to send three regiments of British cavalry, with so inadequate a force of infantry, and no artillery except a detachment from Gibraltar, illustrates the complacent optimism prevalent at Whitehall. While ministers were dreaming of a push forward to Lyons, they neglected to send the arms and the men necessary for the defence of Toulon, or rather they trusted to the Allies to send them. As Hood pointed out in a letter of September 8 to Mulgrave, the most urgent need was the despatch of field officers, an able engineer, artillerymen and two battalions of infantry from Gibraltar. With this estimate Mulgrave entirely agreed. On surveying the outer defences he found one post, that of Ollioules, far too advanced for safety, and advised its withdrawal so as to concentrate the line of defence within practicable limits. To this Gravina, "the Spanish commander on shore," readily assented.

But on September 7, before the withdrawal could be effected, the Republicans attacked the post. As to what followed the reports are utterly at variance. The French Royalists claim that their National Guards held up the whole of Carteaux' army until, their last cartridge spent, they had finally to withdraw. Mulgrave, who was not far distant, says nothing about this Falstaffian performance, but reports that the local National Guards fled and proved to be unworthy of trust; that the defence then rested with the Spaniards, who lost thirty-five killed, twenty-two wounded and sixteen missing before they retired[1]. The French Royalists assign smaller losses to the Spaniards but to their own force thirty-five killed, twenty-one wounded and fifteen missing. Mulgrave was on cordial terms with Gravina, who would be likely to know the truth about this affair. It is also significant that from this time the Allies made little use of the National Guards in Toulon and finally disarmed them. On the other hand among the discredited troops the suspicion spread that the Allies, especially the English, were scheming to retain Toulon for themselves.

The loss of Ollioules was doubly serious, not only as spreading discord among the Allies but because that gorge was the gateway into Western Provence and the valley of the Rhone. So long as the Jacobins held it, they cooped the defenders within a fringe of land around the harbour. On the east of Toulon La Barre's force held them to the posts from Mt Faron to Cape Brun; and he might at any time receive reinforcements from the Jacobin forces holding the eastern part of the County of Nice, from Villafranca to the western slopes of the Col di Tenda in the Maritime Alps. Thus the Allies could not attack Ollioules in force without unduly weakening their eastern front where the situation was always precarious. Nor could they drive back La Barre without endangering the still unfinished works at and behind Malbousquet. To lose that fort meant exposing to the Jacobin cannon the ships in the inner road. To lose the batteries at Cape Brun would equally expose the ships in the outer road.

There were however great possibilities on the eastern front provided that the Austro-Sardinian forces operating near the Col di Tenda and on the Genoese Riviera would make a vigorous offensive. Two courses were open. Seeing that the Republicans west of Tenda now had their rear threatened from Toulon, much might result from a blow at their front either near Tenda or to the west of Nice. Or, again, part of the Allied forces might be detached to the port of Oneglia, where British warships would await them to take them to Toulon. The latter course would enable Hood to drive away La Barre and threaten the rear

[1] Mulgrave to Dundas, Sept. 8.

of the main Jacobin army[1]. Much could be said for either course of action; for the former was safer, while the latter offered more decisive results. The one unpardonable sin was to stand tamely on the defensive, and thus leave the Republicans free to concentrate what force they chose either on Toulon or on the Col di Tenda.

Bold tactics on the part of the Austro-Sardinian army were all the more called for because the arrival of Hood's fleet placed the Republican forces at Nice in dire want of food and supplies, which, after the exhaustion of that neighbourhood, they had drawn chiefly from Genoa, Leghorn or Tunis. Further, the revolt of Lyons against the regicide Republic had compelled Kellermann, commander of the French "Army of Italy" operating in Savoy, to detach twelve battalions of foot, a regiment of cavalry and half of his artillery teams to help in the siege of that city, thereby leaving him too weak to attempt anything of importance against the Alpine passes leading to Turin. Now was the time, then, for the Allies to assume that spirited offensive which, in the opinion of Jomini, would always have been their best policy[2]. Unfortunately, the relations between Austria and Sardinia were strained, chiefly owing to the resolve of the Habsburgs to recover possession of the eastern strip of Piedmont around Novara (termed Novarese) which they had ceded to the sub-Alpine realm in the year 1737. The necessities of the Court of Turin enabled that of Vienna finally to formulate this demand on the understanding that Sardinia should indemnify herself at the expense of the French Republic. It was a case of dividing the bearskin before the bear was shot; and the incipient quarrel about the division lessened the zeal for the hunt. Moreover, as we have seen, Austria was on the trail after less dangerous game, and Sardinia lacked nerves and sinews for the chase[3]. On July 21 Trevor warned Hood that he must expect far less help thence than from Naples; and on August 7 he stated that Devins was unable to act with effect

[1] See Jomini, III, 293–4, *Méms. de Barras*, XIII. Barras ordered the diversion of 4000 men towards La Valette.

[2] Jomini, III, 272, 293; *Dropmore P.*, III, 485.

[3] On June 26, Eden, British ambassador at Vienna, stated that, as Hood's fleet was now in the Mediterranean, Austria would withdraw most of her troops then in Italy, so as to reinforce those about to invade Alsace (F.O. Austria, 33).

owing to the paucity and poor quality of the troops and the incredible abuses of the Commissariat Department, which the King, Victor Amadeus, was too weak to redress. Devins refused to move without the necessary provisions, and these were not forthcoming: the King had raised in all 54,000 troops, but some evil influence marred every effort, infected the rank and file with sickness and discontent, so that fewer than 30,000 effectives remained, and these were fain to rely mainly on the natural strength of their positions[1]. By mid-August Austria had sent only 7500 very indifferent troops to help her ally. Such being the situation Trevor pointed out to the Sardinian Government that, as the capture of Nice in that autumn seemed impracticable, there were many advantages in sending a force by sea to operate from the new base at Toulon against the communications of the French force in the County of Nice; that, on the other hand, the driving back of that force westwards (supposing it to be possible) would result merely in concentration of all the strength of the Republicans against Toulon. This argument, for all its cogency, seems to have made no impression at Turin and Tenda.

As the Anglo-Sardinian treaty of April 25, 1793, stipulated the maintenance of a Sardinian army of 50,000 men, Hood despatched to Turin Lieutenant Cooke of the 'Victory,' in order to procure immediate assistance. Cooke reached his destination on September 14 and, after conferring with Trevor and the Sardinian officials, they proceeded together to the King's headquarters at Tenda. There they found a state of friction and discouragement unfavourable to active exertion; and, a French attack seeming imminent, the King and Devins both declined to sanction any diversion of force. The King appeared to defer entirely to Devins on military matters, and the General seemed lukewarm about supporting the British at all. Trevor finally made so strenuous an appeal to the King that an order was at once given for the despatch of two Sardinian battalions from the position at Aution[2]. They amounted to only 800 men, but their arrival at Toulon (September 26) on board the 'Leviathan' and the Sardinian frigate 'St Victor,' was of much assistance; for the troops were staunch, and both officers and men

---

[1] F.O. Sardinia, 12, Trevor to Grenville, Aug. 7, 1793.
[2] *Ibid.*, Trevor to Grenville, Sept. 16.

behaved with exemplary loyalty to their British comrades. The same may be said of other Sardinian detachments, which by the end of October raised their numbers to about 1600 men. The arrival of another contingent on November 24 brought the total up to 2470[1].

Far more important support was to be expected from Austria, for the security of her Milanese province depended largely on the firm occupation of Toulon whence all acts of aggression against North Italy could be effectively countered. This consideration appears to have been recognized at Vienna; for on September 24 that Court promised to despatch 5000 troops from the Milanese to Toulon viâ Genoa so soon as a free passage was granted through Genoese territory and the necessary magazines of provisions were ready *en route*[2]. In due course Hood despatched British warships to bring this contingent to Toulon, with what result the sequel will show.

There remained Naples. There the spirited Queen, Maria Carolina, burned with revenge against the Jacobins of Paris, now the boorish gaolers of her sister, Marie Antoinette. The usually spiritless King also longed for the overthrow of Jacobinism which was beginning to infect the Neapolitans. His chief minister, an Irishman, General Acton, was favourable to the Allies. The British ambassador, Sir William Hamilton, was aged and not very active; but what he lacked was more than made up by the youth, beauty and vivacity of his wife, whose influence on behalf of England was exerted on the nervous and excitable Maria Carolina long before Nelson appeared on the scene. He cast anchor in the Bay of Naples on September 11[3]. Hood had despatched him in his beloved 'Agamemnon' on August 25 (that is, four days before the occupation of Toulon) with despatches for Trevor, viâ Oneglia and thence to Naples. Delayed by baffling winds and calms, he chafed at the slowness of his passage to Naples. But already, viâ

---

[1] Revel (p. 152), who then reckons the British at 3350, the Spaniards at 7150, the Neapolitans at 6650.

[2] F.O. Sardinia, 13, Eden to Trevor, Sept. 24, 1793.

[3] Hamilton to Grenville, Sept. 17, which corrects Mr Sichel's estimate (*Emma, Lady Hamilton*, p. 156) of September 4 for the date of Nelson's arrival. The master's log of the 'Agamemnon' for September 17 is "½ past 3 p.m. made sail." Therefore Nelson was at Naples only six days.

Leghorn, the news of the occupation of Toulon had reached that city, throwing the Queen, the Court and Lady Hamilton into ecstacies of joy. Forthwith Hamilton used his influence to procure the speedy despatch of the stipulated force, and they were ordered "to hold themselves in readiness to embark at a moment's warning."

Nevertheless, the influence of Nelson had to be superadded during four days of joyous festivities before the effect of the warning was visible. He had hoped to convoy the 6000 troops direct to Toulon; but news that a French man-of-war and a small convoy were at anchor on the Sardinian coast sent him off thither on September 17. However, he and Hamilton had in person urged Acton to despatch the first contingent at once rather than wait until the whole force was ready. Consequently 2000 Neapolitans with all their provisions, etc., set sail on September 16 on board six of their men-of-war and one transport. Three other battalions were to leave Gaëta on the 17th under the command of Marshal Forteguerri. Unfortunately, neither that officer nor his men had seen active service. Worse still, the instructions issued to him differed from those whereby Ferdinand confided to Hood the entire command of the Neapolitan troops and ships. Consequently, very soon after the arrival of the first two Neapolitan contingents at Toulon, disagreements broke out between them, all the more so because friction had formerly occurred at Portsmouth, when the proud and susceptible Forteguerri arrived there in a frigate and took offence at some action of Hood's[1]. Owing to a heavy gale on September 23–26, the first division of the Neapolitans did not reach Toulon until September 27[2]. "We are now perfectly at our ease" (wrote Hood on that day), "we do not now fear any number [of the enemy]." Unfortunately, for him, there had arrived in the Republican camp a genius whose energy and foresight were to outweigh the tardy and ill-concerted efforts of the Allies.

---

[1] F.O. Sicily, 6, 7, Hamilton to Grenville, Oct. 8, 29, 1793, Feb. 20, 1794. Acton excused the delay on the ground that Hood on August 12 or 13 wrote that he would not need the Neapolitan troops. I have found no letter by Hood to that effect. The third contingent sailed about November 10; the fourth on December 10, under Marshal de Gambs, an experienced officer who had a high reputation.

[2] Adm. Med. (1793), Hood to Nepean, Sept. 26 (P.S. 27th).

CHAPTER IV

THE FLEETS AND THE DEFENCE

THE advent of Bonaparte on the scene (probably on September 16) marks an epoch in the siege of Toulon. Hitherto the artillery fire of the Republicans had been ineffective. Now it was concentrated more and more on the essentials of the defence, viz. the fleet and the la Grasse heights that dominated the inner road from the south. The duel between his batteries and the British fleet opened on September 18. It was a duel, which, in varying phases, was to endure throughout his career[1].

On that day the Republicans opened a heavy and continuous fire from two masked batteries erected behind a screen of pine trees that fringed the north-west end of the inner road. The attack seems to have been a surprise, judging by the emergency measures taken by Hood to counter it. "For the safety of Toulon" (wrote Hood), "and the security of H.M.'s ships under my command against the enemy's getting hold of the heights with which the Road is surrounded, I was compelled to the necessity of employing a number of floating batteries with heavy cannon, gunboats and galleys." He then states that, having no frigates (for these were away on particular services) to cover the small craft, he took some French ones, "thinking it better that they should be sunk or beat to pieces than my own[2]." The chief of these frigates was 'Aurore,' now commanded by Lieut. Inman and a British crew; other lieutenants were appointed by Hood as commanders of sloops for a day; and midshipmen were placed over the smaller craft. Thus, the Toulon dockyard partly made good the gaps in Hood's *matériel*, but the crisis was now to subject his *personnel* to a heavy strain[3]. On the 19th new Republican batteries of two

[1] Early in December General Du Teil took command of the artillery. On and after December 3 Bonaparte signs the bulletins "commandant en second" (Chuquet, p. 322).

[2] Adm. Med., Hood to Stephens, Oct. 7, 1793.

[3] Duro (*Armada española*, VIII, 35) states that on September 18 shot from French cannon *on Mt. Faron* began to hit ships in the inner road. Probably they were from Bonaparte's batteries near Brégaillon. The Allies held Mt Faron and its spurs.

guns apiece plied the ships with red-hot shot, whereupon H.M.S. 'St George' (98) was brought into the inner road and took station as near as she could to the shallow western end, but too far out for any but her lower guns to take effect. Fort Malbousquet also fired on the nearest of the new batteries but apparently without much result. By the evening, however, the vessels and floating batteries (*pontons*) had, to all appearance, silenced Bonaparte's cannon, though one of the gun-vessels suffered so severely that she had to be towed out of range, and then sank, after her crew had left her. On the 20th Bonaparte reached the shore near Brégaillon, opening there his *Sansculotte* battery which, with the others, pressed hard the ships and small craft. Two of the latter had to sheer off, and one of the heavy guns of the 'St George' burst, killing eight men and wounding twenty. By this time the 'Princess Royal' (98) took an active part in the duel at the north-west corner. Her captain, J. C. Purvis, entered the following in his log: "This day has been the warmest the pontoons have had, the enemy firing red hot shot."

On the morrow a severe westerly gale spoilt the practice of the gun vessels and floating batteries. Against these heaving vessels Bonaparte's artillerymen, working from behind their screen of pine trees, had all possible advantages. One of the "pontoons" sank, and even the 'St George' had to slip the springs on her cables. The first of the very many rounds between the Corsican and the British fleet went strongly in favour of the landsman. The many inequalities in the ground on the western side enabled him effectively to screen his works and to extend them daily from Brégaillon southwards towards la Seyne. Moreover, in the sandy soil the balls and bombs of the Allies for the most part buried themselves harmlessly, while his shot repeatedly hulled the ships; and his new batteries were out of range of the Allied guns at Malbousquet. These details are of more than local importance. As he witnessed the steadily growing supremacy of his cannon over the enemy craft, his nature, always singularly tenacious of first impressions, acquired the conviction which was destined ever to obsess his imagination, that the land dominated the sea.

Such was the cardinal fact of the situation at Toulon; and it was now clear to Hood. The events of the 20th were so alarming as to dispel his usual optimism. On that day he sent Rear-Admiral Sir Hyde Parker to warn Mulgrave (whose despatch of September 26 thus describes the situation):

that several men had been killed and wounded on board the men of war and gunboats, and that the batteries from the shore produced such an effect as to give ground to apprehend that the Road would not be tenable for the fleet if the enemy should take possession of the forts of l'Éguilette and Balaguier, the guns of which had been removed, but the batteries not occupied or protected, the left of our line of defence extending at that time no further than Fort Malbousquet. I should have been from the first [adds Mulgrave] very desirous of possessing the heights of la Grasse had I been in greater force; but, not having considered the fleet as in any danger, I had left that point vacant till reinforcements should arrive, as it is not necessary to the immediate defence of Toulon, and the great extent of our necessary posts allowing scarcely any repose to the officers or soldiers of our little army. Upon the representation made from the commander-in-chief, it became absolutely necessary to collect a force to occupy la Grasse[1].

This passage, now printed for the first time, proves not only the urgency of the crisis, but that Mulgrave (as also Hood) had seen the importance of la Grasse heights. That indeed was but natural; for their steep western declivity dominated the west of the inner road, while their lower ridges, sloping east towards l'Éguillette and Balaguier, commanded the unprotected batteries at those points. Therefore the force occupying the heights would at once be able to dominate the inner road, and, before long, drive the fleet from the outer road. It is, therefore, clear that the importance of la Grasse position was not a secret divined solely by the genius of Bonaparte (as has often been claimed), but had been discerned by the Allies, who, but for their scanty numbers, would have occupied it from the outset. The defenceless state of that commanding promontory seems also to have attracted the attention of certain officers in the Republican forces at Ollioules, before the arrival of Bonaparte[2]. But up to the time of the advent

---

[1] H.O. Mil. Med. (1793). The above passage is omitted from Mulgrave's despatch as printed in *London Gazette* of Oct. 23, 1793.

[2] See Cottin, pp. 208, 209; but he wrongly states that Mulgrave early in September took steps to fortify the heights, and thus gives an incorrect impression of the fighting on September 21. Fox (ch. III) well discusses the special merits of Bonaparte and points out those of Marescot, who arrived on November 24 "pour diriger le génie." See too Professor Spenser Wilkinson in *Owens College Historical Essays*, pp. 453–94; Rose, *Life of Napoleon*, I, ch. iii.

of the little Corsican no one had concentrated effectively on that position. Carteaux was distracted between it and the desire to take the Pomets Fort on the north[1]; and, as he dissipated his forces on both places, he took neither. But, though Bonaparte could not direct the larger operations, yet, within four days of his arrival, he so far menaced the ships as to shake the confidence of Hood.

Mulgrave, thus warned, took immediate action, and his measures were so timely and judicious as to postpone the evacuation during the space of three months. Under cover of darkness he withdrew from Toulon and the fort of la Malgue detachments of 350 Spanish and 150 British troops, embarked them on boats of the fleet and conveyed them across the mouth of the inner road. Landing them at Balaguier Point about 2 a.m. of September 21, he marched on and before dawn occupied the nearest and lowest of the ridges which form the Grasse heights. Acting under Colonels Echavara and Brereton (of the 30th regiment) the little force protected their front with trunks of trees. They had formed a rough breastwork when, about dusk, about 700 Republicans advanced against them, their design being to seize the Balaguier and Éguillette forts and then bring up guns to drive the Allied fleets from both the outer and inner roads. Such was Bonaparte's plan; but Carteaux, always jealous of his influence, sent under Delaborde a force far too weak to carry out so ambitious a programme[2]. The Allies stoutly beat off these assailants with the loss of twelve killed and twenty-four wounded, and Delaborde made no further effort.

At dawn of September 22 the Allies pushed on to occupy the highest crest above la Seyne. There they constructed a work which they armed with 24-pounders. Captain Charles Tyler and Lieutenants Serecold and Brisbane of H.M.'s frigate 'Meleager' directed the hauling of these guns up steep slopes by our indomitable seamen, and soon put the entrenchments beyond reach of a *coup de main*[3]. Bonaparte was furious at the failure of his scheme and exclaimed: "The enemy have seen the insufficiency of naval gunnery: they have risked everything, have made a

---

[1] Colin, *L'Éducation de Bonaparte*, pp. 180–3.
[2] Chuquet, p. 180, reckons it at only 400 men.
[3] *Mems. of Admiral Sir C. Tyler*, p. 40.

successful landing, and there they are with cannon, a covered way and palissades; they are going to receive considerable succours; and we must make up our minds for a siege[1]." At first, however, the position was very weakly held. Mulgrave's report proves that, after the repulse of the French attack, Echavara wished to evacuate the breastwork, and was prevented solely by the firmness of Brereton. Gravina thereupon replaced Echavara by a more spirited commander. Apart from Echavara's *bêtise*, the affair had been admirably carried out. Mulgrave's promptness in throwing troops from the east to the west of the harbour, the secrecy and despatch of the naval service, and the repulse of the French, constitute a model of what a combined operation should be. The importance of the new post led to the adoption of several schemes for its defence, the result being (as Revel observed) "a monstrous creation, to which the freakishness of different fancies had contributed: it was called Fort Mulgrave by the English, San Ludovico by the Spaniards, *le petit Gibraltar* by the French[2]."

Foiled in their attempt to seize the Grasse heights, the Republicans once more had recourse to artillery. The duel of September 18–21 was renewed. While drafts from the ships were sent ashore to help fortify Fort Mulgrave, the 'Princess Royal,' 'le Puissant,' a Spanish ship and smaller craft engaged the enemy batteries on the western shore and bombarded la Seyne. On the 24th the 'Princess Royal' was hauled across the harbour to the south-west end. On the 26th her fire and that of a Spaniard silenced a new battery near la Seyne and partly destroyed that village. On the 27th Hood stated that the ships had three times totally destroyed the French works, but this cheery estimate was based on the tales of deserters. His losses, amounting to nine killed and thirty-four wounded, included those caused by the bursting of a big gun on the 'St George.' On the 29th Captain Purvis of the 'Princess Royal' noticed the enemy working at a new battery between the windmills on the hill to the west of la

---

[1] Chuquet, p. 181.

[2] Revel, p. 142. Mulgrave's despatch shows that he at first took post "on the lowest and easternmost knoll," not on the western and highest point, as is stated by Fortescue, IV (I), 162. Mulgrave moved forward to the western height after the engagement and constructed the work there.

Grasse. It was a sign that Bonaparte was beginning to push on his works round that height with the intention ultimately of crushing Fort Mulgrave by concentric fire, a scheme favoured by the broken ground which screened his guns from those of the Allied shipping. The arrival of Neapolitan and Sardinian troops, however, on September 27 induced in Hood a feeling of complete security. His optimism was shared by Mulgrave, who on September 27 wrote home in these terms: "After the confident manner in which I have ventured to assure you that no impression was likely to be made on our posts, inadequately garrisoned as they were by our original small body, I need hardly express the comfortable security I feel with our last reinforcements[1]." In view of the marked superiority of the Allied troops over the Republicans, the confidence of Mulgrave was natural; but so emphatic an expression of it induced at Whitehall the conclusion that all was well at Toulon and other objects might therefore receive more attention.

In point of fact the Allied forces at Toulon were always in danger. Bonaparte's last move had compelled them to spread out their forces far more widely; and most of the troops which arrived on September 27–28 were too unsteady to be of real service. The strain upon the British therefore continued unabated, and with the advent of autumn rains it told heavily on the best troops, who perforce were kept at the outposts. Bonaparte's artillery heavily plied the ships in the inner road, and on the 30th 'l'Aurore' was so badly hulled as to be withdrawn. The 'Princess Royal' bore the brunt of the fighting near la Seyne until November 5 when she too was withdrawn. The craft helping her in October were the French 74 'Puissant,' a bomb frigate, pontoons and gun-vessels. Help was also given by two Spanish bomb-vessels which arrived on September 29; but, if we may judge by the logs of the British ships, the Spanish fleet as a whole was of slight assistance. The following, taken from Nelson's letters of October 7 and 11 at Toulon, are of interest:

Our situation here is wonderful: the hills are occupied by the enemy, who are erecting works for mortars and cannon. Whether we shall be able to maintain our most extraordinary acquisition,

---

[1] *London Gazette*, Oct. 23, 1793.

time only can determine; however one hour will burn the French fleet....The Spaniards behave so infamously that I sincerely wish not one ship or soldier was in Toulon: they will do nothing but plunder and cut the throats of poor wretches who have surrendered to the British.

On October 11 (perhaps owing to the arrival of a large contingent of Neapolitans on October 8), Nelson hoped that the whole of that coast would fall to us, as all the population hated the National Convention.

During the sixteen weeks of the Allied occupation of Toulon, Nelson was only five days (Oct. 5–10) in that roadstead and was never on shore, though a party from the 'Agamemnon' was sent ashore to help in the defence. These facts alone would reveal the variety of duties which fell to Hood's lighter craft. They had to escort victuallers or patrol the neighbouring coasts, hunt down the foodships bringing supplies to the Republicans at Marseilles and Nice, and, in general, knit together an otherwise loose and helpless confederacy. It is not surprising to find Hood complaining that he was nearly blinded by his correspondence. It may be well briefly to describe here the more important of the services now rendered by the fleet.

Pressing requests had come to Trevor at Turin, Drake at Genoa, and to Hood at Toulon, for aid to the Royalists of Corsica. Rallying at the call of that picturesque patriot, Paoli, they had overcome the Republicans so that by September 1793, only three strongholds, S. Fiorenzo, Calvi and Bastia, flew the tricolour. A Captain Masseria, partly in British pay, now came to beg help from the British forces, and his promises of easy triumph won ready credence from Hood's manly optimism. Accordingly, on September 8, the Admiral instructed Commodore Robert Linzee to proceed with a squadron, first to Villafranca, the port of Nice, and endeavour to persuade some French warships stationed there to declare for Louis XVII, an appeal which they indignantly refused. Thence he was to make sail for Corsica. Linzee in the 'Alcide,' with another 74, the 'Courageux,' the 'Ardent' (64) and two frigates, 'Lowestoffe' (*sic*) and 'Nemesis,' failed to induce the garrison of Calvi to hoist the *fleur de lys*, and then coasted along to the Gulf of S. Fiorenzo. At the head of that deep inlet he

attempted to reduce the redoubt of Fornili opposite the town of
S. Fiorenzo; but, the wind failing, the ships could not occupy
favourable positions off Fornili, and were badly raked by the
town's guns which had been reported to be too light to carry so
far as the ships. The loyal Corsicans also failed to attack the
redoubt from the land side; and Linzee was compelled to draw off,
after losing sixteen men killed and thirty-nine wounded, and sus-
taining much damage aloft (October 1). The affair heartened the
Republicans and disgusted the British with the loyal Corsicans.
Hood admitted that he had "received no one Instruction about
Corsica, and my sending the squadron thither was a spontaneous
action of my own[1]." He probably knew that Corsica entered into
the plans of the British Government, but to send it early in
September, while drafts from the fleet were urgently needed for
the defence of Toulon, is a proceeding open to criticism. Hood
soon had reason to distrust both Paoli and Masseria, and he described the former as "a composition of art and deceit."

The British Admiral next turned his attention to the nominally
neutral Republic of Genoa. As has already appeared, the French
frigate 'Modeste' and two tartans had insulted and molested
H.M.'s frigate 'Aigle' in the harbour of that city. The Genoese
Government ignored the matter, as also the seizure by those
vessels of a Marseilles tartan, 'Notre Dame de Grace,' which had
gone to Genoa with a safe conduct from Hood. As Francis Drake,
our envoy at Genoa, failed to exact any reparation from that
Government, whose conduct in allowing supplies of corn to go
through to the Republican armies was notorious, Hood resolved
to end this intolerable situation; and he did so with characteristic
vigour. On September 26, that is, two days before the arrival of
the Neapolitans, he ordered Rear-Admiral Gell in the 'St George'
to proceed to Genoa with three 74's, 'Bedford,' 'Captain,'
'Scipion' (French), and the smaller craft, 'Mermaid,' 'Tartar,'
'Alert,' 'Speedy,' 'Éclair,' 'Vulcan' and 'Conflagration.' On arriving there he was at once to assure the surrender of the
'Modeste,' the two tartans and other French ships. He was also
to instruct Drake to demand from that Government satisfactory
assurances for the future, or, in default of them, to blockade

[1] Hood to H. Dundas, Oct. 27, 1793. See Appendix E. H.O. 28 (vol. 14).

the Genoese ports and coast[1]. The Grand Duchy of Tuscany having also acted in a manner detrimental to the Allies, Gell was to proceed to Leghorn, capture the French Republican frigate, 'Impérieuse,' there in harbour, and instruct Lord Hervey, British envoy at Florence, to demand the expulsion of the French Jacobins from Tuscany.

Accordingly Gell proceeded to Genoa. The first to enter the harbour was the 'Bedford' (Captain Man). As to what followed accounts vary. The master's log states:

October 6 [5] at Genoa; prepared to board the French frigate. The Captain warned her not to resist: some of their crew jumped overboard; short struggle on the frigate. 'Modeste' (36) taken, 275 men; also two tartanes.

Reports received by Trevor state that

as soon as the 'Bedford' took her station near the 'Modeste,' and while the fort was saluting the Rear Admiral, all the French crew came upon deck and behaved with so much insolence both as to language and gestures that Captain Man immediately fired into her with small arms and afterwards boarded her and took possession of her, sword in hand; many French are said to have been killed in this affair.

Drake in a letter to Trevor merely stated that Gell, by Hood's order, seized the 'Modeste' with the two tartans and that two men were killed on these last[2]. French versions give the number of their casualties either as five killed, thirty wounded, or from forty to fifty killed[3]. To try to snatch the truth from this bubbling hotchpotch is futile. What is certain is that Hood's highhanded reprisal for the original insult threw the Francophils of Genoa into transports of rage and led to a heated correspondence between the British and Genoese Governments. Drake declared that the British fleet would blockade Genoa. But the Senate, hard pressed by French demands for reparation, and threatened with a declaration of war by the French commissioners at Nice[4], finally decided to expel all foreigners but French. Drake thereupon embarked on Gell's squadron which blockaded all the Genoese coast and captured neutral vessels bound thereto. All relations were

[1] Instructions of Sept. 26 to Gell (see Appendix E).
[2] F.O. Sardinia, Trevor to Grenville, Oct 7.
[3] Cottin, p. 172 note. James's account (1, 96) is inadequate.
[4] *Ann. Reg.* p. 185.

broken off; and, among other untoward results of the rupture, Genoese territory could no longer be used for the embarkation of the 5000 Austrian troops from the Milanese expected at Toulon. The conduct of Genoa had been irritating, but the imperious conduct of Hood, Gell, Man and Drake precipitated a rupture which, with patience and tact, might have been avoided. It was of the first importance to get the Austrian troops through to Genoa or Savona as quickly as possible for the defence of Toulon. Now the only port available was Leghorn. The Bay of Vado was thought of, and on October 23 the 'Windsor Castle' with four Neapolitan and one French craft and thirteen transports cast anchor in that bay in hope of embarking them[1]; but, as they did not arrive, the squadron made first for Spezzia, then Leghorn[2].

Meanwhile, on the Grand Duchy of Tuscany the threat of naval coercion had been successful. Hearing that British warships were about to visit the port of Leghorn, and, terrified by the protests of Lord Hervey against its recent confiscation of corn belonging to merchants of Toulon, the Grand Duke hastily complied with our demands and expelled the French embassy and its adherents (October 8). Nevertheless three British 74's proceeded to Leghorn, according to order, and remained there or off that coast some time, doubtless in order to enforce the new regulations. The French 74, 'Scipion,' which remained there, took fire and blew up. The evidence pointed to incendiary action, probably by prisoners taken from 'la Modeste' who had been put on board: 150 of the crew perished.

During the whole of October the strain on the fleet was very great. As has already appeared, Linzee's action off S. Fiorenzo had badly damaged his ships, which had to refit at Cagliari. On October 7 he wrote to Hood requesting that four or five ships should cruise off C. Corse to cut off supplies intended for the French garrisons in Corsica; but no ships were available. On October 27 Hood wrote to the Admiralty stating that, as the

---

[1] Log of the 'Windsor Castle' (App. C).
[2] Hood to H. Dundas, Nov. 24, 1793 (App. E). Austria at once made the excuse that, until the Genoese dispute was settled, she could not leave Lombardy unguarded, and therefore could not send the 5000 Austrians formerly promised for Toulon. Sir Gilbert Elliot thought the rupture with Genoa a mistake (*Elliot, Life*, II, 183 note).

'Courageux' had been on shore in Corsica, and the 'Robust' was without a mainmast, he actually had only one 74 at Toulon fit for sea, viz. the 'Captain'; but he was daily expecting the 'Fortitude,' 'Colossus,' and 'Leviathan' from Leghorn. Of course he had the three-deckers, the 'Victory,' 'Britannia,' 'Princess Royal'; but the 'St George' was off Genoa and did not return to Toulon until November 10; the 'Windsor Castle' sailed thence on October 17 to escort the transports to Vado Bay for the long expected Austrian troops. In view of the aggressive attitude of the Spaniards, who kept their fleet concentrated at Toulon, Hood's situation was highly critical. The 'Diadem' (64) from England joined the flag on November 19, but on December 14 left with the 'Tartar' to observe Genoa.

The arrival of British reinforcements was prominent among the cares and anxieties of Hood. Unfortunately, ministers at home believed the situation at Toulon to be so favourable as to call for no immediate succour. They had planned to send by sea 5000 Hessians from Flanders; but, on September 25, Austria promised to send instead 5000 troops from her Milanese province to Toulon, because "it would be more advantageous to the common cause, and more expeditious, to send 5000 Austrians, instead of the Hessians, who might be employed on the Rhine or in the Low Countries[1]." Relying on this explicit promise the British Government withheld the Hessians as well as reinforcements from these islands; but Sir Robert Boyd, Governor of Gibraltar, received orders to despatch to Toulon as many troops as possible. Though Spain was now an ally, and the Brest fleet was a negligible quantity, he nervously refused to send more than 750 men, and among them very few of the gunners that were urgently needed. To the intense disgust of Hood, who had sent the 'Terrible' and 'Egmont,' and the frigate 'Iris' to carry or escort the hoped for reinforcement, those ships returned on October 27–28 with that scanty succour along with General O'Hara. Thereupon, on November 1, Hood wrote to Boyd a letter of remonstrance, pointing out that 1500 good troops arriving a week earlier would have done wonders (*i.e.* in the fighting of October 29); and he besought him to despatch every man that could be spared from the Rock by the

---

[1] F.O. Austria, 34, Eden to Grenville, Sept. 25.

ships now about to sail for that purpose, viz. the 'Egmont,' 'Colossus,' 'Fortitude,' 'Ardent,' and the French sloop 'Moselle.'

Meanwhile, a further complication had occurred. On October 26 Hood received from the Admiralty an order, dated October 1, instructing him to remove the soldiers of the 30th regiment, serving as marines on the 'Princess Royal,' 'Robust,' 'Terrible' and 'Alcide' on to the 'St George' and three other sail-of-the-line, despatching them to Gibraltar under the command of Rear-Admiral Gell, with the intention of sending them to the West Indies. The cause of this extraordinary proceeding clearly was the very optimistic estimate of Mulgrave as to affairs at Toulon in the early part of September. Further, by that time invitations had reached Whitehall from French Royalists in the West Indies offering to put the chief French colonies into British hands. The offers were tempting[1], but in reality the last place to be depleted of troops was Toulon. Hood and Mulgrave now saw that fact. On October 26 they wrote expressing deep concern at the serious losses which obedience to the new orders must entail. The orders, however, were positive. Owing to the remonstrances of Hood and O'Hara, and the absence of the 'St George' on the Genoese coast, Gell seems not to have sailed from Toulon until November 21, and, along with the 'Colossus,' he reached Gibraltar on the 30th (the 'Fortitude' and 'Leviathan' arrived five days later). There he received the Admiralty's secret instruction of November 15, ordering him to return at once in the 'St George' with the 74's and rejoin Lord Hood's fleet.

This singular *volte face* at Whitehall obviously arose from the belated discovery that Mulgrave's and Hood's roseate reports of the situation at Toulon in September were fallacious. Awakening from their fools' paradise, ministers now hurried back to Toulon the troops they designed for conquests in the West Indies. But the change came too late. Owing to inexplicable delays the first part of Gell's squadron did not set sail on its return voyage till December 9. Colonel [Sir] John Moore, who with the troops embarked on the 5th, deemed the delay very strange. Perhaps it resulted from the late arrival of the 'Fortitude' and 'Leviathan' on December 5. But as the master of the 'Fortitude' then

---

[1] Rose, *Life of Pitt*, II, ch. ix; *Dropmore P.*, II, 395, 438, 443, 444, 454, 464.

reported—"Found 'St George,' 'Colossus,' 'Egmont,' 'Ardent,' three Portuguese men-of-war, and several frigates" at Gibraltar, it is difficult to see why some of these sail were not used for the transport of troops known to be very urgently needed at Toulon. Gell's letter of December 9 to the Admiralty shows that he appreciated the need of despatch, for he said that he would send the two regiments on warships as being faster than transports. But Moore's diary gives the impression of leisurely arrangements on his ship, the 'Egmont' (Captain Dickson). Not till after hearing news of the reverse at Toulon on November 30, were there any signs of expedition on board. Perhaps, however, the delays were due to slackness on shore, where the dockyard people were far from smart, and an inadequate water supply often hindered ships. However that may be, the 'Egmont,' 'Colossus,' 'Fortitude,' 'Ardent,' and the sloop 'Moselle,' did not sail until December 9. The frigate, 'Ariadne,' sailed that same day, and, being fast, reached Toulon on the 16th in time for the fifty artillerymen on board to be of service in the fight of the 17th. The others, delayed by the bad sailing of 'Moselle,' hove in sight of Toulon ten days too late[1].

It is difficult to conceive a more fatal series of blunders than those which are here described. The resolve to withdraw troops from Toulon, and then to send them back again, the delay in shipping them piecemeal from that port, their straggling arrival at Gibraltar, the leisurely arrangements for their return, and the clogging of the squadron by a wretched little lame duck, involve discredit on everyone concerned. The result of these fatuities was that the 'St George' and 'Leviathan' were detained at Gibraltar, and four sail-of-the-line with two regiments on board were crawling back to Toulon, while the fate of that stronghold was being decided by a genius who knew the value of time and concentration of energy[2].

The weakness of Hood's fleet at the crisis of mid-December resulted from the diverse duties then pressing upon him. Among these was the bringing of Maltese seamen consequent on an agree-

[1] Adm. Lords' Letters, Gell to P. Stephens, Dec. 9; *Diary of Sir John Moore*, I, *ad init.*

[2] On January 1 Gell transferred his flag to 'Leviathan' and sailed for home on January 10 (Captain's log of 'Leviathan').

ment with the Grand Master of the Knights of St John. For that purpose Hood despatched to Valetta the 'Captain' about November 10. 'Aigle,' 'Aimable' and 'Modeste' were there with her in December–January on the same errand[1], which had the effect of depriving the Allies of four crews at the time when the blow fell.

We must also glance at one more ex-centric effort, due to the need of gaining over to the Allied cause the Bey of Tunis. From that port many food-ships proceeded to Marseilles or Nice intended for the French armies outside Toulon or in the Maritime Alps. As the defence of Toulon turned largely on cutting off the food supplies brought to the besiegers by sea, it was necessary to intercept those which came from Tunis. Hood, on entering the Mediterranean, had despatched a letter to Magra, British consul at that port, urging him to win over the Bey, but, owing to the presence at Tunis of a French squadron of superior force, that letter was not delivered. True to his original scheme of sweeping up every French ship in the Mediterranean, Hood desired to send to Tunis Commodore Linzee with the squadron under his command off the coast of Corsica. But, the operations at Mortella and S. Fiorenzo having badly damaged some of those ships, Linzee was unable to move for some time, and had to send the 'Courageux' back to Toulon for repairs. In mid-October Hood ordered the 'Berwick,' 'Illustrious' and 'Agamemnon' to join Linzee at Cagliari; and on November 15 he instructed him to proceed to Tunis with the 'Alcide' and the ships above named, also the frigates 'Nemesis' and 'Lowestoft,' for the purpose of cutting out the French squadron consisting of 'Duquesne' (74) and four frigates destined to convoy French merchantmen to Marseilles. The frigates, however, had put to sea and on October 22 had a sharp brush with the 'Agamemnon' off Sardinia, finally putting in to S. Fiorenzo, and strengthening the Republican garrison. Hood seems not to have known of the sailing of the frigates. At any rate he adhered to his design of inducing the Bey to adopt the Allied cause. Linzee was to remonstrate with that potentate on his partiality for the French, "who are daily committing murders that would disgrace the most savage of the human race[2]."

---

[1] Captain's log of 'Captain.' 'Aigle' sailed on January 1, the others later.
[2] See Appendix E.

The Bey was moved by the display neither of superior morality nor of superior force, and Hood finally opined that his obduracy was due to the arrival of a Spanish squadron which must have sown the seeds of jealousy against England. Seeing that Linzee had to do only with one French 74, Nelson was disgusted that he did not carry her off by force and thus end the affair at once. But Hood's instructions were definite. He forbade Linzee to offend the Bey, as his friendship might be very serviceable. It is not easy to reconcile this deferential attitude, when we had an overwhelming superiority of force, with Hood's masterful policy of July. Clearly Nelson was exasperated at our tame proceedings; for he thus summed up the affair—"We English never yet succeeded in a negotiation against the French; and we have not yet set the example at Tunis." To sum up; four sail-of-the-line and one or two frigates were employed up to the beginning of 1794 in trying to gain over the Bey and to prevent the sailing of 'Duquesne' and her convoy[1].

On the whole, these ex-centric operations were ineffective and produced a lamentable dispersion of the British fleet. Against one success, in Tuscany, there must be set three failures, at S. Fiorenzo, Genoa and Tunis. The results in the case of Genoa were especially serious. General Dundas, writing on November 22, about the food supply at Toulon, says: "Almost everything must come by sea, and such resource at this season of the year is very precarious, and from Genoa at present we can have nothing. Bread and vegetables while they last are the great support of the multitude. Meat is 14d. per lb., and the smaller articles are proportionately dear[2]." The rupture with Genoa also detained a British squadron off that port, besides hindering the embarkation there of the 5000 troops so long promised by Austria.

---

[1] Extracts from log of 'Berwick': "Dec. 29.—Arrived 'Nemesis' from Toulon bringing news of evacuation. Jan. 2, 1794.—Weighed anchor with 'Alcide' and 'Nemesis,' leaving 'Illustrious' and 3 Spanish sail of line and 1 frigate." The 'Agamemnon' was at Tunis nearly the whole of November.

[2] H.O. 50, 455.

CHAPTER V

THE EVENTS OF OCTOBER AND NOVEMBER

WE return now to a brief review of the struggles on shore in October and November, 1793. On the night of September 30–October 1, Lapoype, who succeeded La Barre in command of some 6000 Republicans on the east of that city, sent three columns, in all about 1700 strong, to assail Mt Faron. That of the right, under Victor (the future Marshal under Napoleon), scrambled up the almost inaccessible goat track, the *Pas de la Masque*, and at dawn surprised at the summit a picket of sixty men who immediately retired to a redoubt at La Croix de Faron. This "they found abandoned by the Spanish garrison without firing a shot[1]." The other French columns coming up from the east, the whole summit was very soon in the hands of the Republicans, probably without the loss of a single man. Fort Faron (on a lower spur) being in great danger, Captain Elphinstone, R.N., sent Captain Torriano with ninety-two men of the 30th regiment as a reinforcement, and Mulgrave despatched Captain Beresford of the 69th regiment to enable Elphinstone to make a diversion on that side if occasion offered.

A council of war having meanwhile resolved on the recapture of the mountain, Mulgrave took command of 300 Sardinian and 250 British troops attacking from the St Antoine redoubt on the west; Admiral Gravina's column, consisting of 400 Neapolitan grenadiers, 183 Spaniards, besides some Sardinians and French Royalists, was to ascend the southern slopes by the Valbourdin dip. Before setting out the troops saluted the Bourbon white flag, now for the first time officially hoisted over Toulon. As usual in emergencies Hood landed seamen from the fleet to take the place of the soldiers sent forward.

Both columns breasted the precipitous slopes without opposition, save that 200 Republicans at the crest opened a distant and harmless fire on Mulgrave and then hastily retired. Captain

[1] Mulgrave to Dundas, Oct. 3 (*London Gazette* of Nov. 16).

Moncrief pushed on with an advanced guard and occupied the top of the *Pas de la Masque*. The French, though now reinforced from below, retired along the undulating ground towards the highest and easternmost crest where stood the redoubt of La Croix de Faron. Its present defenders, apparently, had no artillery available and the two Allied columns advanced unopposed over very difficult ground, converging as they neared the highest ridge, until, on arriving almost within charging distance, they halted to recover breath. Elphinstone, meanwhile, very judiciously advanced a column of some 530 Allied troops up the south-eastern slope to threaten the enemy's left flank somewhat in the rear, while Gravina menaced its front. The Republicans, now about 1800 strong, held the summit, their right wing being protected by the precipice on the north, and their right centre by a ravine, which, beginning in the northern height, descended sharply towards Toulon, leaving on the north at the summit only some twenty paces of level ground. Noticing, however, that the enemy's left (drawn back *en potence* at the wing) was so perched on the top as not to command the ravine in its front, Mulgrave rapidly conferred with Gravina, and it was agreed that the latter should use the cover of the steep slope to ascend near to the enemy's line, whereupon Mulgrave's column was to charge. Very skilfully these tactics were carried out. Elphinstone's men, now led by Colonel del Porto, also ascended on their side and contributed in no small degree to shake the defenders. Preceded by an intrepid Spaniard, Serjeant Moreno, Gravina's force crept towards their objective, whereupon all three columns charged home.

In advance of the British in Mulgrave's force strode a Highland gentleman, Thomas Graham of Balgowan, whose fury against the Republicans was now about to be appeased. Several months previously his beautiful wife died of consumption in that same Riviera; and while he was conveying her remains across France to his northern home for interment, the coffin was torn open by a Jacobinical rabble intent on unearthing a conspiracy. Thenceforth he pondered on revenge. The outbreak of war and the sailing of Hood's fleet for the coast of Provence afforded him the opportunity; and, as a volunteer, he was foremost in many an exploit at Toulon, as he was ever to be foremost, until his fiery spirit and natural genius for war brought him, full twenty years later, across the Pyrenees into the plains of France, as General Graham, Baron Lynedoch, the greatest of Wellington's lieutenants.

Preceding even the ardent Captain Moncrief and the Sardinian officers, Foras and Revel, Graham led the charge across the narrow neck at the summit. In vain did the Jacobins ply their musketry against these determined assailants. The Sardinians and British were not to be denied, and drove in the French right wing. Farther down the slope the short sharp frontal attack of Gravina crumpled up the French left, while Elphinstone pushed on del Porto's force uphill against its flank and rear. He covered the ascent by the fire of twelve-pounders from Fort Faron, directing the gunners to plant their shot about fifty yards in front of the column, and, when necessary, to stop their *barrage*—probably the first use of this device. Thus protected, del Porto's men soon dislodged the Republicans from the south-eastern edge of the summit while Gravina's men crushed their front. Abandoning the redoubt, the Republicans rushed in confusion northwards, only to find their comrades there thrown back by Mulgrave. Finally the jostled mass made for the precipitous northern slopes, down which it was hurled by the converging pressure of the Allied assault. Many fell into the abyss, many more were killed or wounded by rocks and stones loosened in that headlong flight. The Republicans left behind on the summit 75 dead and 61 prisoners, but not more than 400 rejoined Lapoype below. Out of a total of 1700 the Allies lost 11 killed and 71 wounded, the heaviest casualties being among the gallant Sardinians. On them Mulgrave both publicly and privately bestowed very high praise; he also warmly commended the steadiness of the British as also of the Neapolitan grenadiers in this their first battle; but his private comments on the Spaniards (excepting Gravina and Moreno) were scathing[1].

The affair was undeniably brilliant, the Allies driving from a strong position a superior force of between 1800 and 2000 troops of the line consisting of the flower of the "Army of Italy." Mulgrave and Gravina displayed dash and good judgment in utilising

---

[1] Mulgrave's and Elphinstone's letters of Oct. 3 and Revel correct Cottin's narrative at some points.

the inequalities of the ground during the final advance, and Elphinstone's timely despatch of 530 men from Fort Faron sufficed to bar the retreat of the enemy where it would have been easy. On the other side the defenders of Mt Faron first neglected the opportunity of defeating Mulgrave's and Gravina's columns while they were separately toiling up the declivities, and maintained an equally tame defensive at the crisis. Further, neither Lapoype nor Carteaux seems to have made the slightest attempt at a diversion[1]. In fact the Allies, both leaders and rank and file, outclassed their opponents, and proved that, with anything like an equality of numbers, the defence of Toulon was assured. The victory was marred by one unfortunate circumstance. Gravina received a wound in the leg which incapacitated him during several weeks. Thanks to his tact and courtesy the question of the supreme command of the troops had hitherto been unimportant; for he was content to share it loyally with Mulgrave. Now, however, all was changed. In his place came Brigadier-General Izquierdo, who was so carping and obstinate as at once to irritate "the difficult and haughty character of Lord Mulgrave[2]." Their friends had to intervene so as to prevent an open breach, but until Gravina returned all union between British and Spanish ceased.

Another success was gained on the night of October 8–9 by a force of 225 British troops under Captain Brereton, 150 marines under Lieutenant Serecold, R.N., and drafts from the Allies. It captured the nearest Republican battery, spiking the guns, and averting for the present all danger from Fort Mulgrave and the fleet[3].

Less favourable were the next affairs. On October 14 the Republicans between la Rivière Neuve and Ollioules were noisily celebrating the capture of Lyons, the news of which had lately arrived. As their movements seemed to promise an attack on Fort Malbousquet and neighbouring posts, Mulgrave sent out a patrol of 100 men of the 11th regiment under Captain Wemys, who came into collision with parties of the enemy, and, putting them to flight, rushed on in pursuit. Seeing them endangered by

---

[1] Chuquet, p. 298; Fox, p. 27.   [2] Revel, p. 148.
[3] *London Gazette* of Nov. 10; Nicolas, I, 331; Fox, p. 28.

their *élan*, Mulgrave sent forward fifty Piedmontese chasseurs to relieve them, and when Carteaux launched an attack at the reinforcement, larger bodies of the Allies rushed forward to save their comrades. In the scrambling fight which ensued the Allies lost about four killed and thirty wounded. Tactically the skirmish was a mistake, but it proved the superiority of the best Allied troops.

Part of Lapoype's force next attacked an unfinished battery near Cape Brun held by 250 men of the Royal-Louis regiment. Though succoured by 200 British from Fort La Malgue, the Royalists were overborne by numbers and had to retire. Mulgrave then ordered an attack with the view of seizing the heights of Thouars and if possible the village of la Garde so as to cut off the Republicans. This incisive plan was marred by the slow moves of a body of Spaniards, owing to whom the Jacobins escaped inland, abandoning for the time la Valette. Lapoype's intention had been to seize Cape Brun, fortify it, and threaten the British fleet in the outer road, a plan complementary to that of Bonaparte on the west of Toulon. Thus, up to mid-October the Allies had held their own, beating off the attacks both on the west and east which threatened the fleet, while their secure hold on Mt Faron enabled them to separate Carteaux and Lapoype and render communication slow and difficult between those commanders.

But now came a series of untoward events which strengthened the Republican and weakened the Royalist forces. The fall of Lyons on October 9 enabled the Jacobins to despatch large forces towards Toulon; and the failure of Devins' army in an attack on the Republicans in the Maritime Alps on October 18–19 precluded all hope of a diversion from that quarter and virtually ended that campaign[1]. Further, owing to the non-arrival of trustworthy reinforcements, the constant strain on the best of the Allied troops produced sickness and nervousness, in which all differences tended to produce suspicion and animosity. The Toulonese complained that no use was made of their National Guards, whom the Allies distrusted as cowards or traitors. The poor quality of the Spanish troops and all the Neapolitans, except the grenadiers, earned the contempt of the others, while the British were disliked for their insular reserve and arrogance. Only between the islanders and

[1] Krebs et Morris, *Campagnes des Alpes*, I, App. pp. xcix–cii.

the men of Piedmont were the relations friendly and intimate, Mulgrave ascribing the imprudent advance on October 14 to their "affectionate emulation." Occasionally, however, the Sardinians complained that they were being unduly sacrificed[1]. Nor were bickerings confined to officers: the troops quarrelled, especially when means of shelter and supplies of food failed. In this respect the Republicans suffered equally, perhaps worse, Bonaparte himself contracting a malarial fever; but among the Allies the worst troops remained in the town, while the best suffered exposure at bleak outposts on the hills. On October 21 Mulgrave complained that the men on Mt Faron still had short allowances, and those at Malbousquet had received none for two days. When provisions did come, they were very bad, "the meat stinking and the bread full of maggots." What wonder, then, that the numbers of sick steadily increased. Out of 16,912 Allied troops on the rolls at the end of October, barely 12,000 were fit for duty.

Reinforcements of 927 infantrymen and 100 artillerymen arrived from Gibraltar on October 28. They were commanded by Major-General O'Hara. He superseded Mulgrave who now returned to England, his command at Toulon having been only temporary; but he considered that his services had not been duly appreciated[2]. O'Hara was his senior both in rank and in age, and his knowledge of Spanish also marked him out for this command. As the Spaniards persistently claimed priority, Hood informed Langara that George III had sent a commission appointing Major-General O'Hara "Governor of Toulon and its dependencies, and Commander of the Combined Forces." This information drew from the Spanish admiral a spirited protest, on the ground that the Spanish Government had sent out Don Valdez as commander-in-chief.

An examination of this dispute would be wearisome, and it must suffice to state that Hood maintained his former claims, but begged Langara not to compromise the defence of the place by proffering demands which could be settled only by their respective

---

[1] Revel, p. 150.

[2] Letter of November 26 to Wyndham. See also his reports on the condition of Toulon, in Appendix F. Mulgrave reached London on November 23, and the news which he brought for the first time alarmed Pitt and Dundas (*Dropmore P.*, II, 471).

Governments[1]. This was the right course to take, and Pitt and Grenville fully endorsed his claim of British supremacy at Toulon. Fortunately Gravina recovered sufficiently to resume his duties, whereupon Anglo-Spanish relations became less strained. His affability won all hearts. He approved of Captain Sir Sidney Smith commanding the Spanish gunboats; but, for some reason, that arrangement did not take place.

On October 27 there arrived at Toulon from England viâ Genoa, Major-General David Dundas (1735–1820), a distant relative of the politician, Henry Dundas, but by no means intimate with him. He had seen much service and was highly versed in strategy and tactics, being counted the most scientific and learned of British officers. He therefore brought to the defence what had hitherto been lacking, a trained and mature intelligence; but unfortunately he came too late to amend the defects in the Allied positions and fortifications; and his disposition was so desponding as to overrate difficulties and somewhat depress the spirits of the garrison.

Both O'Hara and Dundas took an extremely serious view of the situation. On November 11 O'Hara drew up for Hood an alarming statement (see Appendix E). It set forth the very great difficulties of the defence, naming, *inter alia*, the poor quality of most of the troops, the obstacles to communication by water during bad weather with the troops on the la Grasse heights, the risks of standing on a mere defensive, and the need of an advance inland to drive the enemy from their now fortified positions. All this was true. Yet it was not the whole truth[2]. If communication was often difficult with those heights, it was still more difficult between the two French armies of the east and the

---

[1] See Hood's and Langara's letters in Cottin or in the *Naval Chronicle* for 1799. On November 10 Hamilton at Naples wrote to Grenville that the King of Spain had lately written to the King of Naples reproaching him "for the trust His Majesty has reposed in Lord Hood by giving H. Lp. the entire command over his sea and land forces, and that probably he would have reason to repent so rash a measure." Hamilton informed Hood of this. (F.O. Sicily, 6.)

[2] Revel (p. 156) states that O'Hara presented only the difficulties; but these should not daunt them. The 5000 Austrians might come, and then Sardinia would send 10,000 men, and an offensive could be made. Anyhow, it would be shameful to withdraw. Hood and Elliot heartily welcomed these views.

west, and if the Allied forces present had been efficient and trustworthy, they would have sufficed to crush either of those isolated
forces. O'Hara was right in deciding to await the arrival of
British and Austrian reinforcements, and he strongly deprecated
the withdrawal of the 30th British regiment. It sailed for
Gibraltar, however, on November 21.

Wherever the best of the Allied troops were attacked, they gave
a good account of themselves, as in repulsing an attack on Fort
Mulgrave on the evening of November 15. The assault was said
to be due to the indignation of the Republicans at seeing the
Spaniards in the fort maltreat a French prisoner; they rushed
forward, but were received with a hot fire and fell back. Bonaparte led up supports, but they were beaten back by those of the
Allies. O'Hara had been on the 'Victory,' but, hearing the firing,
he hurried to the fort and valiantly headed a sortie of British and
Neapolitans which repulsed the Republicans with heavy loss.
Thereupon, the new commander, Doppet, ordered a retreat. According to French deserters the fire of the ships' guns and of the
fort did much execution, so too did the explosion of a powder
magazine in their rear. Bonaparte's fury against Doppet perhaps
hastened his recall. He, a physician, had just replaced the painter
Carteaux; now, on November 16, there arrived at the headquarters
at Ollioules, a warrior both by nature and training, Dugommier.
With him there came General Du Teil to take command of the
artillery from Bonaparte, and, a few days later, seven battalions
marched in from Lyons, and seventeen from the army of the Alps.
Guns and munitions poured in[1]. The arrival of these formidable
reinforcements and the non-arrival of the forces so long expected
by Hood tilted the balance heavily against the defenders.

Civil affairs had also been complicated by the arrival, in mid-
November, of Instructions from Whitehall instituting as Royal
Commissioners for the control of Toulon "and its dependencies"
Hood, O'Hara, and Sir Gilbert Elliot. The last named (afterwards
first Earl of Minto) had latterly had several conferences with
ministers, and, leaving London about October 20 and Genoa on
November 9, landed at Toulon on the 19th. Thenceforth, as
Governor, he administered civil affairs, relieving Hood of part of

---

[1] Chuquet, p. 198. See also his *Dugommier*, chs. 4, 5.

the excessive burden which had overstrained his strength[1]. Pitt had insisted on the appointment of a British Governor "in consequence of the place being surrendered to us[2]." The stiff attitude taken up by ministers was probably due to two considerations. Firstly, they were resolved to exact a suitable indemnity from France for her aggression against us, and Toulon would form a guarantee for the exaction of such an indemnity. Secondly, they were resolved to exclude from Toulon the Comte de Provence, who desired to come thither in the self-assumed character of Regent for his nephew, Louis XVII. It soon transpired that Spain was supporting the demand of the Toulon "sections" on behalf of the Prince and worked energetically on his behalf. Not only the British officials but Revel believed the Spaniards to be privy to this plan, the success of which (so he wrote) might seriously harm the Allied cause[3]. This was probable enough; for, besides leading to the interference of the Prince in military affairs, where unity of command was essential, his arrival would attract to Toulon a swarm of waspish *émigrés*.

A firm tone therefore characterized not only the British Instructions but also the British Declaration which Elliot read out to the Toulon authorities on November 20. As some of its phrases caused a painful impression, he altered them; *e.g.* instead of Toulon being "surrendered" he substituted "entrusted" (*confié*). He changed the fourth article considerably, because of its liability to misinterpretation, and the doubtful character of the present situation. His modifications averted all chance of a rupture with the Toulonese; and, after conferring with them, he strongly advised the admission of the Regent to Toulon. The Ministry, however, had firmly vetoed this proposal, instructing Drake at Genoa in the last resort to warn the Prince that he would not be allowed to land at Toulon[4]. On technical grounds, they had some justification for their conduct. In his Declaration of August 28 Hood stated—"I take possession of Toulon and hold it *in trust only* for Louis XVII, until peace shall be re-established in France." But by the constitution of 1791 the Comte de Provence had no

---

[1] *Elliot, Life*, II, 187.
[2] *Dropmore P.*, II, 447.
[3] Revel to Monsieur, Nov. 27 (Turin Archives).
[4] F.O. Genoa, 20, Grenville to Drake, Oct. 22.

legal claim to the title of Regent for Louis XVII, and that claim
was denied by very many Royalists. Further, Hood and the
British Government were the fiduciary possessors of Toulon during
the war, and could alone decide as to its administration. Nevertheless, it must be admitted that the exclusion of the Comte de
Provence, though justifiable on legal grounds and for military
reasons, was a highhanded proceeding. Fortunately, the question
did not come to an issue. The leisurely progress of the Prince and
the rush of events at Toulon averted what would have been a
singular scene at Genoa. He was travelling through North Italy
when the news reached him of the Republican triumph at Toulon.

In passing we may notice the bland assumption of ministers,
that Toulon "and its dependencies" were firmly enough held to
form a guarantee for the exaction of an indemnity at the peace;
also the signal folly of requiring Elliot to make known their
expectations. They had also persuaded themselves that Toulon
had absolutely surrendered to Hood, though his Declaration and
despatches gave no warrant for such an assumption. Further, it
led them to treat what was a sacred pledge as an article placed in
pawn which might be retained until their further claims were
satisfied, a course of conduct which would have been a breach of
faith. It is, however, an exaggeration to assert that they con-
templated the annexation of Toulon. For the Instructions of
October 18 made it clear that the indemnities in the south of
France could be found only in districts "contiguous to the frontiers either of Spain or of Sardinia or possibly of Switzerland,"
and that no extensive projects of aggrandisement were contem-
plated by the British Government. Nevertheless, the use of the
term "surrender" as applied to Toulon gave some colour to the
charges now circulated by the Spaniards and others, that England
intended to make of it a second Gibraltar. The incident therefore
annoyed the Toulonese and exacerbated our relations with Spain.
The Commissioners ventured to exceed their Instructions in regard to conciliating the Royalists of Toulon, and they decided to
admit a detachment of armed *émigrés*, but this help was to arrive
too late. At this time there was every need to conciliate the
Toulonese; for, by some *bêtise* on the part of Langara, an important secret had leaked out, that Spain had sent him secret

instructions as to the eventual removal of the French ships. The news caused intense irritation, being naturally regarded as a proof of perfidy on the part of the Allies, and it sensibly diminished both their influence and the desire of French Royalists to fight for them[1].

Meanwhile the duel between the ships and the batteries had led, in general, to the discomfiture of the ships. Captain Purvis notes that his ship, the 'Princess Royal,' was often hulled, sometimes by 44 lb. shot. On November 3 a red-hot ball did much damage and burnt the deck as it rolled about, until a seaman caught it in a bucket and threw it overboard. Two days later the ship was ordered to move out of range; but on the 12th, finding that the enemy's largest gun still sent balls over his masts, he moved the 'Princess Royal' farther east. Even then several shot passed over her, the gun (a long 44 pounder) having a range of at least three miles[2]. Floating batteries and bomb- and gun-vessels were the best means of replying; but the want of them was still severely felt. On this subject Captain Sir W. Sidney Smith, R.N., made some interesting comments.

This enterprising free-lance had been on a political mission to Turkey, and, after the outbreak of war with France he proceeded to Smyrna, where, finding forty English seamen, he induced them to come with him on a small vessel, the 'Swallow,' which he bought. Joining Hood at Toulon, he made her over for service as a guard-vessel in the inner road, and then offered to equip a flotilla from similar craft in Toulon dockyard. His offer was declined, greatly to his surprise, for the fleet badly needed vessels that could do harbour and coast service without constantly putting back to port. For lack of such craft the Allies could not stop the coastwise traffic from Marseilles or Italy which still brought supplies to the Republicans. The shells recently thrown against Fort Mulgrave (says Smith) came by sea, the heavy ships of the Allies being helpless to intercept the polaccas and luggers that carried them[3]. With his natural bent for guerrilla methods, Smith depreciated the work of sail-of-the-line, asserting that the

---

[1] F.O. Spain, 28, St Helens to Grenville, Oct. 30.
[2] Log of 'Princess Royal' (see App. C).
[3] S. Smith to Lord Auckland, Dec. 12, 1793 (*Auckland Journal*, III, 153).

'Princess Royal' during three weeks had been firing at a two-gun battery,

without making any impression on the heap of sand of which it was formed, while every shot from the shore struck some part of her rigging or hull....Line of battle ships are very useless machines in this war, now that there are no line-of-battle ships of the enemy to fight....*Small* vessels with heavy artillery are the only species of force that can act with advantage on a coast or cooperate with an army. I now repeat and offer to prove my assertion[1].

There is much force in Smith's contentions; but, as usual with him, he injured his case by exaggeration, also stating that captains refused to admit the advantages of a flotilla of gun-vessels because of the hardships which such service involved. This motive would have weighed neither with Hood nor his captains; but it is possible that the admiral erred in not giving free play to Smith, an ideal leader for such work. Thus, for lack of a light mobile force, the Allies failed to stop the coasters that brought Bonaparte much of his ammunition, and his guns steadily gained the superiority over the ships and floating batteries in the inner road. By comparison with this fact the arrival, on November 12, of 3786 Neapolitan troops was of little importance, but there was hope of reinforcements both from Gibraltar, Ireland, and the Milanese. Hood therefore held on, undismayed by the increasing difficulties of his situation.

It is often stated that Bonaparte's efforts were concentrated against Fort Mulgrave; but Du Teil and he by no means neglected the direct method of attack, viz. upon Fort Malbousquet. Bonaparte's bulletin of November 29 records a heavy day's work between the Allied fort and ships and the French battery *la Convention*, which fired regularly upon the fort, apparently disregarding the ships. South of it Bonaparte was pushing on two batteries, *la Farinière* and *la Poudrière*, the latter being ready on the morrow to open on Malbousquet with four guns and three mortars[2]. Its fire taking effect even on the city of Toulon and the arsenal, O'Hara determined to carry the work by a night attack,

---

[1] S. Smith to Lord Auckland, Dec. 12, 1793 (*Auckland Journal*, III, 153).
[2] Chuquet, p. 321. His narrative (pp. 207–9) errs by describing the Allied attack as on *la Convention*. The accounts of Hood and Elliot both state that it was on the new battery (*la Poudrière*).

like that which had succeeded so well from Fort Mulgrave on October 9. His scheme was carefully thought out. Seamen were landed from Hood's already depleted crews to hold a position whence O'Hara withdrew the garrison, 400 men of the Royals. Sardinian, Neapolitan and Spanish detachments brought the total up to 2300 men, who took station at and north of Fort Malbousquet and moved into the valley at 4 a.m., the British being on the left. The surprise was almost complete; the Republican division of some 6000 men defending la Poudrière offered a very weak resistance and then broke and ran; farther north, the Allies occupied la Farinière, possibly also la Convention. Unluckily the British, carried away by their elation, now broke ranks and rushed after the flying enemy, "like so many foxhounds" (wrote Hood), for the space of a mile. The natural result followed. The other detachments moved forward in a disorder which gave the beaten enemy his chance. From rear and flank he sent up reinforcements, which, using the vineyard walls and other obstacles, shattered the pursuit and drove it back in rout.

O'Hara, realising the crisis, rushed forward to rally his men. It was in vain: the Republicans swarmed up, cut off parties of the Allies, and wounded O'Hara, so that, collapsing under a wall, he fell into their hands. On the right Revel had kept his Sardinians in comparative order, and now defended the bank of the river long enough to enable British gunners to work their guns against the Republican masses. Coolly and accurately the gunners mowed down the pursuers, who also suffered heavily from the enfilading fire of the ships in the north-west arm of the harbour. All their efforts to rush Malbousquet (which was open in the rear) were beaten back with losses, which Dundas reckoned at four to five hundred killed. The British lost twenty killed, eighty-three wounded and ninety-two prisoners or missing; the other contingents, except the Sardinians (who lost 100 men), suffered less[1].

The annoying thing about the affair was that, if the Royals

---

[1] Hood to H. Dundas, Nov. 30 (see Appendix E); Revel, pp. 158–61; D. Dundas to H. Dundas, Dec. 2 (Adm. H.O. 50). Revel says the French at the close of the day "faisoient un feu terrible sur les troupes et sur les artilleurs Anglois, dont la constance et l'adresse sont dignes de toute l'admiration" (Revel's *Relation*; Turin Archives).

had been less spirited, the day would have been won; or, on the other hand, if their headlong pursuit could have been followed up by equally good troops, the Allies might have captured Ollioules with the headquarters, stores and ammunition of the Republicans. As Marescot, commanding the Jacobin engineers, exclaimed—"What would then have been the fate of the Republicans!"[1]

[1] Moreau de Jonnès (whose *Mémoires*, compiled in 1809, have been translated by Brig.-General A. J. Abdy) states that O'Hara came with 7000 troops to surprise the battery of Les Arènes. Equally mythical are his statements that an Anglo-Spanish Commission sent prisoners to the gallows; that 11,000 English soldiers fled into Toulon on Dec. 18; that they repelled refugees from the boats, while the Spaniards welcomed them, and so on.

CHAPTER VI

THE FINAL STRUGGLES AND EVACUATION

THE affair of November 30 by no means rendered the defence hopeless. The Allies had inflicted heavier losses than they sustained, and had once again displayed their decided superiority in *moral*, 600 of them having at first routed 6000 Republicans, who, even when reinforced, failed to break the thin line of the defence under Malbousquet. Dugommier manifested extreme disgust at the unsoldierly conduct of the French, and made the almost incredible statement that they fired off 500,000 cartridges[1]. Certainly, they proved themselves to be excitable, disorderly and untrustworthy. Indeed, it is worthy of note that, not until the crisis of December 17 did the Republicans fight well; and their success then was due probably to the new troops lately brought up.

Moreover, O'Hara was no great loss. Revel ascribed to him all the soldierly qualities except those needed for a commander-in-chief[2]. Elliot, who saw more of him, was less charitable, asserting that his strange, rattling way of talking, his excitable manners and persistent pessimism aroused much apprehension. "The night before the action" (wrote Elliot), "he was as nervous as it is possible to conceive, and was wretched about the whole business and its possible issue." Elliot then describes his successor, General David Dundas, as old, of infirm health and depressed spirits, and desirous of being relieved of his responsibility, but sensible and steady by comparison with "his harum scarum predecessor[3]." Dundas took the same desponding view of the situation as O'Hara, and advised Hood to evacuate Toulon while he could do so without difficulty; but the admiral "chose to follow his own opinion[4]."

The whole problem turned on the arrival of reinforcements of trustworthy troops. Five thousand of the splendid Austrian troops whom Mulgrave had admired in passing through Tyrol,

[1] Chuquet, p. 210.
[2] Revel to Monsieur, Nov. 10 (Turin Archives).
[3] *Elliot, Life*, II, 195.
[4] *Diary of Sir J. Moore*, I, 41.

or three or four thousand British troops from home, or in part from Gibraltar, would have sufficed to assure the possession of Toulon. Again, if Hood could have retained with the flag the four British sail-of-the-line and two frigates that were at Tunis, and the two squadrons which twice sailed on their vain quests to Vado or Gibraltar, drafts of seamen amounting probably to 2000 men would have been available for service on shore. Hopes of reinforcement from Gibraltar rose high on December 16, for early on that day there arrived from the Rock the frigate 'Ariadne,' bringing not only a captain and fifty artillerymen but the longed for news that two regiments were being hurried thence to Toulon and that the abandonment of the expedition to the West Indies would liberate other troops for the coast of Provence. Hood, who was now living on shore, was so excited by the news that he ran to inform Elliot: "I never saw a man more delighted than Lord Hood" (wrote Elliot). "He came skipping into my room, out of breath with hurry and joy[1]."

Far different was the reality. Owing to the discreditable delays at Gibraltar, the two regiments arrived off Toulon nearly a fortnight after its evacuation. Thus owing to the delays of Gell's squadron (or of the authorities at Gibraltar) and the absence of other squadrons on particular service, the number of British ships with the flag at Toulon was perilously small. On the critical day, December 17, H.M.S. 'Terrible,' 'Robust,' and 'Courageux' (the last under repair), with the frigates 'Ariadne' and 'Nemesis,' appear to have been the only British craft (apart from gun-vessels) in the inner road[2]. The 'Princess Royal' was near the exit, and the 'Victory,' 'Britannia' and 'Windsor Castle,' with the frigates 'Romulus' and 'Sincere' were in the outer road. But this was little more than one-third of Hood's fleet.

The last considerable reinforcement to arrive was a body of Neapolitans on December 5; but these were unseasoned troops of little value. Their commander was an Alsacian, General Gambs, whose reputation as a soldier stood high[3]. He was appointed to command all the Neapolitan troops at Toulon, but he had no

---

[1] *Elliot, Life,* II, 199.
[2] Logs of 'Victory' and 'Princess Royal' (Dec. 17).
[3] F.O. Sicily, 6, Hamilton to Grenville, Oct. 8.

time in which to imbue them with his energetic spirit. Another misfortune for the Allies was the increasing alienation of the Toulonese. It was due in part to the refusal to allow Monsieur to come to Toulon, but also to the growth of that national sentiment which always asserts itself when strangers meddle in domestic feuds. Such intervention always strengthens the party of resistance, and a score of incidents every day helped to turn the townsfolk against the foreigners. The bad conduct of the local National Guards caused annoyance to the Allies, whose contempt of those runaways was answered by hatred. At last, in the second week of December, Hood, Dundas and Elliot decided to disarm and deprive of their uniforms the town troops, and to withdraw from the batteries all the local cannoneers. Revel commended these precautions against treachery[1]; but these events bred suspicion, estrangement and exasperation.

On the other hand national sentiment increased the zeal of the besiegers. They strained every nerve to recapture Toulon, and their forces were formidable by their weight. The chief difficulty was to maintain discipline and to provide the necessary rations. So far back as November 13 the *représentant en mission*, Fréron, wrote from Marseilles to his colleagues urging them to send supplies of food; for "We are always on the verge of collapse.... All the corn of *ci-devant* Provence is exhausted. The armies devour it. You must send corn in all haste from all the Departments where the harvest has been good. You know how hunger favours the hopes of our enemies[2]." The memoirs of de Revel also show that in December the Republican forces were in such grave difficulties for want of food, that they must strike a successful blow or else decamp. The Committee of Public Safety had sent to Dugommier the suggestive message "Vous prendrez Toulon, ou vous mériterez nos regrets[3]."

In the miserable condition of the French roads, large supplies, whether of munitions or food, could reach the besiegers expeditiously

---

[1] Revel to Monsieur, Dec. 12 (Turin Archives).
[2] Chuquet, p. 298. See Fox, App. II, for Barras' final plan of attack.
[3] Revel, p. 164. On January 4, 1794, Giacommazzi, Venetian resident at Turin, informed his Government that they need not fear an immediate French invasion of Italy, as Provence was swept bare of food (Venetian Archives).

only by the River Rhone and thence by coasting vessels to some
bay west of Toulon. As we have seen, the Allies failed to stop this
source of supply, and the Republicans thus secured enough stores
to warrant the venture of a final effort. Their 40,000 men now
threatened all points of the Allied perimeter and left it in doubt
where the chief blow would fall. In order to strengthen Fort
Malbousquet the Allies began to work at a redoubt a little to the
rear on the Missiessi hillock; but the works were much hindered
by the Republicans in the Poudrière and Farinière batteries, the
latter of which was complete by December 8. Bonaparte thus
menaced Toulon with direct attack; but meanwhile he was pushing
on his redoubts to the south of Fort Mulgrave: the *Jacobins*,
Hommes sans Peur, and *Chasse-coquins* redoubts, which opened
fire on December 15 or 16[1]. In all eight batteries now directed
their fire on Fort Mulgrave. The losses they sustained from the
guns of the fort and the floating batteries were severe, but the
best gunners were stationed at this post of danger, and the words
scrawled by Junot on a signpost—"*Batterie des Hommes sans
peur*" forbade all thought of shrinking. Bonaparte himself concentrated on Fort Mulgrave a fire of great intensity, as many as
seven bombs being seen in the air at once[1].

Neither ashore nor afloat did the Allies make an effective reply,
the fleet having been too weakened by the diffuse operations
previously described either to send large drafts ashore or enfilade
the *Chasse-coquins* and *Sans Peur* batteries. As we have seen,
Captain Sidney Smith was convinced of the uselessness of heavy
ships against the Republican batteries at Toulon; and his dictum,
that "small vessels with heavy artillery are the only species of
force that can act to advantage on a coast or co-operate with an
army[2]," was certainly applicable to the conditions at Toulon.

Finally, the defences of Fort Mulgrave had been laid out on
no systematic plan by one skilled engineer, but incoherently by
amateurs; and their execution by the Spanish General Izquierdo
had been halting, his artillery colonel being fully occupied at Fort
Malbousquet. The works were still going on when interrupted by
the heavy bombardment of December 15–16; and, according to
Revel, the front had no protection either by a ditch or by effective

---

[1] Chuquet, pp. 205, 206.   [2] *Journal of Lord Auckland*, III, 153.

obstacles[1]. The upper part of the fort was strong and commanding; but the strength of a work is that of its weakest part, and that part, on the right or western end, was decidedly weak, besides being easily accessible by a rush from a short distance. This section was held by Neapolitans and Spaniards. Fearing an attack on this important and unfinished fort the Allies despatched thither a reinforcement of 350 men, but it proved to be inadequate. The defenders also possessed no light cannon for the defence of this portion of the work, and the heavy pieces on the parapet fired so slowly as to be of little use in an affair at close quarters.

Against a garrison of some 700 men, of whom about 250 were British, there moved three columns comprising 7000 men, of whom 4000 were picked troops. Mustering at la Seyne after dusk of December 16, the Republicans were delayed by heavy storms of rain, but the feverish energy of Bonaparte brooked no long delay, and at 1 a.m. of the 17th the columns plashed through the streams that coursed down the western slopes of la Grasse. Storm clouds hid the face of the moon, and in the darkness the second column went to pieces, only the steadiest nucleus getting home. These men and those of the first column overpowered two outposts of British and Spaniards, who were cut to pieces or retired to the fort. The garrison could open fire only at close range. At the left, held by British and Piedmontese, the assailants forced their way in, only to be driven out twice. Then Dugommier sent for the third column held in reserve by Bonaparte. Headed by him and Muiron, it came on and attacked both the left and the right of the work. Meanwhile the Spaniards posted on the right, having received a reinforcement of fifty-eight Piedmontese and thirty-six British, had held their ground; but the onset of fresh troops broke their defence. Thereupon Conolly, Captain of the 18th (Royal Irish) regiment sent in all the British reserve, which for a while held the Republicans at bay, until, as their numbers grew, panic seized on the Spaniards who turned and fled. Before the increasing stream, the British and Piedmontese had to give ground, and about 4 a.m. Conolly and the Chevaliers de Napion and de

---

[1] Revel, pp. 164–8. French accounts speak of *chevaux de frise*, etc., but these can have been only very partial.

Beauregard led the survivors in a gallant and successful effort to cut their way through to safety.

Meanwhile, General Izquierdo with a body of Spaniards posted lower down on the east, half way to Fort Balaguier, had not advanced to their succour; and, though Dundas and Gravina promptly sent in 400 men by boat, yet they arrived too late to be of service. Thereupon Izquierdo declared that with them, he would retake the fort, but no one trusted a man who had not moved forward at the crisis[1]. The reinforcement, however, availed to hold the Republicans in check on the Grasse heights. Hood, with his usual hopeful pugnacity, opined that the fort might have been retaken, for on December 20 he wrote:

> The enemy declined to follow the combined troops, who retreated to the next hill, and [the enemy] having destroyed a great part of the fort they had taken possession of, retired for a considerable time; but, there being a want of spirit and vigour to retake the post, the enemy took courage and in the afternoon came on again in great force, which occasioned a total evacuation of all the heights and a retreat to the boats.

This judgment differs utterly from that of General Dundas and the soldiers, who saw that the loss of the fort involved an immediate evacuation of the peninsula.

If any doubt remained on that subject, it was ended by another untoward event, the loss of Mt Faron. There a detachment of Spaniards, posted at the head of the very precipitous Pas de la Masque, was surprised by the eastern Republican army, which pressed on and, despite a brave resistance by Piedmontese and British pickets, captured the heights. As many as 313 British (officers, N.C.O.'s and men) were killed, or wounded, or made prisoners in the fighting there and at Fort Mulgrave. Of these casualties the marines accounted for sixty-two, and the seamen

---

[1] Revel (p. 169) says "qu'on pouvait accuser Izquierdo de la perte de Ft. Mulgrave." Captain Purvis of 'Princess Royal' notes in his log of Dec. 17, "The Neapolitan camp, consisting, together with the reinforcement from the town, of about 1500, kept the enemy at a stand till about 7, when it was determined to withdraw all the troops from that post."

I have found no good plan of Ft. Mulgrave. Those re-produced by Cottin, Krebs et Morris (*Campagnes des Alpes*), and in the Barras *Mémoires* are misleading. General Dundas wrote of it that "no part of this *temporary post* was such as could well resist determined troops."

twenty-nine. The exhaustion of the British and Sardinian troops rendered inevitable the evacuation of Toulon. A decision to that effect was arrived at in a Council of War held under the presidency of Lord Hood on the afternoon of December 17. There were present Langara, Gravina, Dundas, Valdez, Pignatelli, Forteguerri, Hyde Parker, Revel and Elliot. As there remained in Toulon only 1500 effectives, the recovery of the posts just abandoned was deemed impracticable, but, according to Revel, Hood still opposed the evacuation of Toulon and desired to await the arrival of the reinforcements daily expected from Gibraltar, as well as those from Piedmont and the 5000 Austrians. Revel, when asked his opinion, replied in favour of evacuation, adding, "Milord, all Europe knows that it was you who took Toulon, but nobody can accuse you of having lost it[1]." Finally, it was decided to evacuate the outer forts and posts, and to concentrate the troops at Artigues, St Catherine's, Malbousquet and Missiessi, these being held as long as possible in order to cover the withdrawal. The Toulonese were to be warned to leave if possible on the merchantmen in the harbour, receiving, however, "every possible assistance in provisions, etc., and every other facility." The sick and wounded were to be embarked at once, and the French men-of-war that did not sail away with the Allies were to be burnt along with the stores, etc., in the dockyard. On these questions the council of war decided unanimously. Such, too, was its vote for the abandonment of the Cepet Peninsula—a more debateable topic, decided in the affirmative, apparently, on the advice of the officers of engineers, d'Aubant, Pozzo, Maturina, and the commander of the artillery, Captain Collier[2].

The details of the evacuation and of Sir Sidney Smith's attempt to destroy the French warships and stores in the dockyard have been so often set forth that it is unnecessary to describe them in detail. The difficulty inherent in these very complex operations was increased immeasurably owing to a panic which seized the

[1] Revel, p. 172. Duro (*Armada española*, VIII, 37) states that Gravina alone favoured another attack, which he offered to lead. Neither the official account nor that of Revel mentions this.

[2] I have not found their report. Revel (p. 170) includes Izquierdo, Allavida and Buèler, as present at the council of war, and he omits Elliot. I have adhered to the official account.

Neapolitan garrison of the Missiessi battery; their defection un-
covered the flank of Malbousquet, and a night attack of the
French drove out the Spaniards who were holding that important
work. From these two points of vantage the Republicans began
to bombard the town, into which the Neapolitans and Spaniards
began to pour in disorderly throngs; but the bombardment somewhat disconcerted the Jacobinical element among the inhabitants.

  In order to expedite the escape of the Toulonese Royalists, the
embarkation of the troops was fixed for 11 p.m. of December 18;
also an embargo was placed on all private shipping so as to reserve it for the refugees. But these plans were marred by the
inrush of Neapolitans, first from Missiessi and not long after
from Artigues and St Catherine's forts which they also abandoned.
The Spaniards from Malbousquet joined them and added to the
crush and panic in the town. Following the example of flight set
by Forteguerri and Pignatelli, the Neapolitans crowded to the
quays, seizing much of the shipping, and (says Elliot) firing on
boats of refugees that refused to take them. Consequently the
escape of the Royalists and the work of withdrawing the sick and
wounded, numbering over 4000 (Revel says 6000) was greatly
impeded; but the latter task was finished on the 18th. The same
authority states that many Toulonese escaped on the boats that
were removing the sick and wounded. He, however, asserts that
no boat from the fleet put in to the quays before 2 p.m. of the
18th, but obviously this was due to their being occupied with the
sick and wounded. The suggestion of sinister motives for this delay
comes with a bad grace from one who had voted in the council of
war that the sick and wounded were to be embarked first, and
that the Royalist inhabitants were to be warned to leave on
fishing or trading vessels. Revel also admits that there were
plenty of fishing or trading boats or vessels on which Royalists
could escape[1]. That very many did so escape is clear from Hood's
journal for December 18, 8 a.m., which runs—"Receiving French
refugee families." The logs of the British ships also show that,
on the 18th, after warping farther out, the crews managed to
rescue very many Toulonese. 'Victory' states—"All employed
receiving French refugee men, women and children." 'Princess

[1] Revel, p. 175.

Royal' states (December 18)—"The poor inhabitants are flocking on board the ships, begging to be received"; and (December 19)—"boats of all descriptions bringing on board emigrants." Elliot estimated the number on board the British ships at about 2000[1]; but in a letter of December 21 to H. Dundas, he says "several thousands[2]." It must also be remembered that the British sail-of-the-line then at Toulon numbered only six, with a few smaller craft, and that some of them, especially the damaged 'Courageux,' needed boats to tow them to the outer road. Three French sail and six or seven smaller vessels, manned by Royalist crews, were also available; but the total number under Hood's command was less than that of the Spanish fleet. The chief responsibility therefore rested with Admiral Langara, and there is no reason to suppose that he or his men shirked it.

Certain French writers, including Thiers, have spoken of the callousness of British officers and seamen towards the refugees. One rumour even charged them with being too occupied with saving their baggage to rescue the Toulonese. Fortunately, this slander can be refuted. Revel states that the Allied troops lost almost all their effects[3]. Dundas, also, in his letter of December 21 says "Embarking all our baggage was out of the question, and therefore everything of a heavy nature was left behind, my own among the rest"; and on January 7, 1794, he writes that the troops "are totally destitute (independent of their personal wants and losses) of every circumstance necessary to take the field." He estimates the personal losses of officers at over £3000, while above 900 men had lost knapsacks and necessaries[4]. It is therefore equally clear that officers and men brought away almost nothing except uniforms and muskets, and that the ships' boats worked hard, first to embark the sick and wounded, and then as many refugees as possible. Hood afterwards wrote (January 1794) that "every inhabitant was brought off as manifested inclination to come" (a statement which is obviously exaggerated), but he added "I most earnestly wish more had done so, from the insatiable revenge that has been taken"—which shows that there

---

[1] *Elliot, Life*, II, 200, 205.   [2] Adm. H.O. 50.
[3] Revel, p. 173. So too the log of 'Courageux' for Dec. 17—"The ship hauling out in a hurry, left coals on shore."
[4] H.O. 50 (Mil. Medit.), D. Dundas to H. Dundas, Dec. 21.

was no lack of good will on his part. As to the number of refugees brought away, the estimates vary very widely. Elliot's estimate of 2000 is far more probable than that of 14,000 later on ascribed to Hood[1]. The French warships brought away about 1500; their merchantmen only 500—a very low total; the Spaniards and Neapolitans altogether about 3500, bringing the grand total to 7500.

The Allied troops, with certain unworthy exceptions, were brought away last of all. In order to avoid congestion in the town, Dundas had arranged with Gravina to embark them, not at the quays or in the dockyard, but in the outer road near Fort La Malgue, a decision which gave the townsfolk a better chance to escape but imperilled the safety of the troops in case an easterly gale rolled in a heavy sea. Fortunately, the weather was calm until the last hour of the crisis; but the situation was infinitely complicated, on the morning of December 18, by the disorderly withdrawal of the Neapolitans. Nearly all their men sailed away without orders[2]. The other contingents for the most part preserved a semblance of discipline, those from the town filing out secretly at night by a postern in the eastern wall, while a rear guard kept up a heavy fire on the hostile garrison of Fort Catherine.

---

[1] James (I, 89) puts the number on the British ships at 15,000, which is impossible, seeing that they were crowded with troops, sick and wounded. He estimates the population of Toulon as 60,000: General Dundas put it at 30,000. He states that a few field guns were got off to the 'Victory' (see his letter of Jan. 22, 1794). Dundas's estimate of the personal losses sustained by the British was too low; for at Bastia on December 2, 1794, Lt.-Col. J. Moore and Major R. Pringle of 51st regiment, and Lt.-Col. S. Wauchope of 50th, certified as follows: "Upon the day of evacuation the British covered the retreat of the army, were under arms from daylight and were marched in the evening...to the place of embarcation. They therefore had no opportunity of saving anything but their arms and accoutrements, with the cloaths actually upon their backs....The numbers entitled to compensation are (N.C.O.'s and rank and file) 2 Batt. Royals 355, 11th Reg., 380, 18th or Royal Reg. of Ireland, 294, 25th, 27, 30th, 278, 69th, 351. Total 1685."

[2] H.O. 50 (Mil. Medit.), D. Dundas to H. Dundas, Dec. 21; *Elliot, Life,* II, 205–6.

Revel (p. 174) states that Dundas tried to arrange for the Spaniards and Neapolitans to embark at the quays and the British and Sardinians from the dockyard, but was resisted by the Spaniards. Dundas's account is as follows: "Having determined with Lieut. Gen. Gravina, that, instead of embarking at the quays and in the arsenal of the town, our whole force should assemble near Ft. La Malgue...." Further, how could the Allies embark in the dockyard and town (on which *un feu infernal* was pouring) when they desired to fire the ships and stores in the dockyard?

Thanks to the staunchness of that guard, the protection of the guns of Fort La Malgue, and the distraction caused by the fire and explosions in the dockyard, the Allied troops were able to reach the open coast near Forts Louis and La Malgue. Among them were the Royal Louis and two independent companies of *chasseurs* raised at Toulon, in all about 600 men, of whose spirit and fidelity General Dundas spoke in the highest terms. Equally warm were his encomiums on Captains Elphinstone, Hallowell, and Matthews, R.N., who contrived to maintain some degree of order at the embarkation.

After dusk of December 19 all the ships' boats put in to the shore near the forts above named; but on that rocky coast the work of embarking some 9000 troops might appal the stoutest heart. At first the northern sky was lit up by the conflagration at the arsenal, soon, however, to be shrouded by a dense pall of smoke. The explosions completed the demoralisation of many of the troops, the remaining Neapolitans for the most part rushing into the water or clambering on the rocks and calling out piteously to the seamen—"Napoli, Napoli." Thanks to the *sang froid* of the Sardinians and British, the confusion was not irremediable. Their rearguards stoutly held the two forts and were ready to beat off an attack; but none was made, either because the Republicans had not detected the retreat or were concentrating their attention on the town and dockyard. Finally, the rearguards spiked the guns of the forts, marched in order to the boats and were embarked without loss. The self-restraint and fortitude of these men, under the command of Major Koehler and the Sardinian officers, is beyond all praise. Had their discipline given way during the long drawn out suspense of that terrible night, a serious disaster must have occurred; for before dawn there arose an easterly wind driving into the bay an ugly swell. By sunrise, however, all the boats had reached the ships, which thereupon began heavily to beat out to sea towards the anchorage of the Hières Islands. The last to leave was the frigate 'Romulus' (Captain Sutton) which covered the last boats and did not weigh anchor until fired at from Fort La Malgue[1].

It remains briefly to describe the efforts of small parties, under

[1] Master's log of 'Romulus.'

the command of Captain Sir Sidney Smith, R.N. and Don Pedro Cotiella, to destroy the dockyard stores and the French warships which the Allies could not bring away. Smith volunteered for this dangerous work, and received energetic support from Captain Hare of the fireship 'Vulcan,' Captain Edge of the 'Alert' sloop, and Lieutenants C. Tupper and J. Gore of the 'Victory,' R. Miller[1] and J. Stiles of the 'Windsor Castle,' and C. Pater and R. Middleton of the 'Britannia,' and detachments from those ships[2]. Their attempts to burn the stores and warships were hindered by the threatening conduct of the Republican workmen and galley slaves, also by the action of the Spanish firing party in blowing up, instead of scuttling, two powder-ships—a blunder (some said an act of treachery) which cost the lives of three British seamen. Nevertheless, Smith and Hare believed that at least ten sail-of-the-line were destroyed as well as the stores of masts, pitch, tar, tallow, oil, ropes and hemp. The stillness of the air, however, confined the fires within comparatively narrow limits; and the destruction accomplished was less than Smith stated in his report, the rope and hemp stores being little damaged before some of the French workmen or galley slaves extinguished the flames[3].

The destruction of the French warships that could not be brought away had been voted by all the Allied officers at the council of war; and, as that action was afterwards to be represented as the outcome of British malice, we may notice that, so far back as October 3, the Spanish Foreign Minister ordered Langara, in the event of abandoning Toulon, to carry it into effect[4]. Hood, however, was informed that the Spanish Admiral was very loath to do so, alleging that "it might be for the interest of England to burn the French fleet, but that it was by no means the interest of Spain." Hood also maintained that "had the Spanish Admiral fulfilled what he engaged to do, the whole would

[1] Lieut. R. Miller commanded H.M.S. 'Theseus' at the Nile, and perished in an explosion off Acre in May 1799.

[2] Others deserving mention are Lieutenants J. Melhuish and R. Holloway of 'Alert,' M. Wrench, T. Richmond of 'Vulcan,' H. Hill of 'Swallow,' J. Priest of 'Wasp,' J. Morgan of 'Petite Victoire,' F. Cox of 'Jean Bart'; midshipmen J. Eales of 'Victory,' R. Hawkins, T. Cowan, W. Knight of 'Windsor Castle,' H. Watson, P. Valliant of 'Britannia,' and Young of 'Union' gunboat (killed), G. Andrews and — Mather of 'Vulcan,' J. Skriner, J. Young, T. Clarke, T. Knight of 'Swallow,' and J. Wilson, "advanced sentinel."   [3] Cottin, p. 335.   [4] Ibid. p. 419.

have been burned[1]." The assertion savours of Hood's hopefulness, and, of course, cannot be proved. Certainly the Spaniards did little towards burning the French fleet, and their chief act, the explosion of the two powder-vessels, injured the British crews more than the French ships; but that incident was probably due to flurry rather than to treachery. Further, the Neapolitans and Sardinians did not help in that work, and, though it was the abandonment of Missiessi battery by the Neapolitans which produced the scurry at the dockyard, they are not accused of treachery.

The French sail-of-the-line burnt at Toulon comprised the following: 'Centaure,' 'Destin,' 'Dictateur' (re-named 'Liberté'), 'Duguay Trouin,' 'Héros,' 'Lys' (renamed 'Tricouleur'), 'Suffisant,' 'Thémistocle,' 'Triomphant.' The 74, 'Scipion,' took fire while at Leghorn. The 80, 'Couronne' (renamed 'Ça-ira'), and the 74's 'Commerce de Bordeaux' (renamed 'Timoléon'), 'Conquérant,' and 'Mercure,' were incorrectly reported burnt. The three last fought against Nelson at the Nile, so did 'Tonnant' (80), 'Généreux,' 'Guerrier,' 'Heureux' and 'Souverain,' which were not injured by fire at Toulon. Four old sail-of-the-line also eluded destruction[2]. A far more important escape was that of the gigantic 'Dauphin-Royal' (*Sans culotte*) then on the stocks, which in 1798 was to be renamed 'Orient' and perish in a grander conflagration! Hood took away with him the old ship on which she was modelled, 'Commerce de Marseilles' (120), as also the 74's, 'Pompée' and 'Puissant'; but only 'Pompée' was found to be fit for active service. Three frigates and three corvettes were burnt by the firing parties. The light craft carried off by the British or captured in neighbouring ports numbered nine; one went to each of the other allies, a share of the spoil which naturally produced some irritation. It is significant that eight out of the thirteen French ships which fought at the Nile were those which escaped destruction at Toulon on December 18–19, 1793. It is therefore clear that, if Sidney Smith had been better backed up by our Allies, Bonaparte's eastern expedition could not have set sail in 1798.

[1] See Appendix E for the letter, dated January 1794.
[2] In the case of each ship which escaped the *Naval Chronicle* (1799, p. 299) adds the comment "Intrusted to the Spaniards to be burnt, consequently saved."

CHAPTER VII

EPILOGUE

"WITH those who acted with us at Toulon, everything was difficult, and every difficulty was insurmountable." This judgment of Elliot's savours of insular pride; but, allowing for the epigrammatic form of the remark, and excepting from its scope the brave and devoted Sardinians, we may endorse it as a suggestive epitome of the causes of failure. Naturally enough, it leaves out of count the deeper causes, political and diplomatic, which men of that day could but dimly surmise. They may be passed briefly in review.

Prussia, sated with the spoils of Poland, viewed with keen jealousy the Habsburgs' plans for "indemnification" in North France and designedly threw on them the chief burden of the war in the west. They therefore declined to divert towards Provence the 10,000 or 12,000 troops which at that time we urgently demanded. Even the promise of 5000 Austrians was made conditional on the surrender of the Novarese by Sardinia, she "indemnifying" herself at the expense of France[1]. The chances of the latter gain being problematical, the House of Savoy rejected the proposal. Thereupon Austria sought to enforce it by starving the war in that quarter; and underneath all the excuses for the non-departure of the 5000 Austrians the disputes between that Court and her Prussian and Sardinian allies were the one efficient cause. The inactivity of the Austro-Sardinian forces on the borders of Nice, after their unsuccessful effort of mid-October, enabled the Republican armies operating in the Maritime Alps to despatch large reinforcements to the besiegers of Toulon. It was these reinforcements which decided the fate of that city.

Thus, the acquisitiveness of the two German Powers reacted in two ways on the defence of Toulon. Prussia's jealousy of the Habsburgs enfeebled their action at all points of the war, and their resolve to secure part of their "compensation" in Italy deadened

[1] F.O. Austria, 34, Eden to Grenville, Sept. 25, 1793.

those military activities on the Riviera and in the Alps which ought to have redoubled the effect of Anglo-Spanish efforts at Toulon. With even a moderate amount of energy, the Republicans should have been overborne both in Flanders and the Rhineland, on the Sardinian and Spanish fronts, and in the local centres of resistance—la Vendée, Lyons, and Provence. We are here concerned only with the last; but it should be remembered that in September–October the Jacobins had seven campaigns on hand. The Allies and Royalists failed in all of them for want of a good understanding and effective co-operation; but the campaign in Provence and Nice had offered golden opportunities. For the Austro-Sardinian forces to push on from the valley of the Var to Toulon was no heavy task; and with mutual goodwill and the help of Hood's fleet in cutting off the enemy's food supplies, it should have been accomplished in a few weeks. Ill-will and bad faith bred procrastination, until the season was too advanced for active operations; and this again enabled the Republicans to strengthen their army to the east of Toulon, with the results that have been seen.

No blame can attach to the British fleet. Hood's conduct of the naval operations erred, if at all, by excess of energy in several parts of the Mediterranean at once. Above all, it was unfortunate that his action at Genoa brought about a temporary rupture with that Republic. But even that set back might have been made good if the Austro-Sardinian army had driven back the half-starved Republicans as it ought to have done. Failing that, a diversion should have been made in their rear by sending reinforcements by sea to the Allies at Toulon. Neither course was adopted. Therefore this campaign, which might have provided an effective instance of naval and military co-operation, remains an example of one-sided and therefore fruitless effort.

On the other hand, the British Government had sought to solve a problem that was virtually insoluble. The protection of the coasts, of commerce, and of the flank of the Duke of York's force in Holland, would alone have strained the strength of a Navy, then very imperfectly manned; but our southern Allies also demanded naval succours. The Admiralty met these demands by despatching Hood's fleet in four sections, primarily with a view to convoy work; and, as we have seen, it arrived in the Mediterranean too late to co-operate with full effect either with the Austro-Sardinian forces or with the Royalists who were seeking to arouse Provence against the Republic. The loss of Marseilles was a serious blow to the monarchist cause, for it closed the gate by which succour could perhaps have been sent through to Lyons. Thereafter the Republicans could isolate the malcontent elements and hope to crush them in detail. It is further questionable whether the Admiralty should not have despatched more light vessels suitable for co-operation with the army of Devins and the stoppage of the enemy's sea-borne supplies of food.

The decision of the Toulonese to entrust their fortunes to Hood was, on the whole, a counsel of despair. It resulted, not so much from the pressure of his naval blockade (as Nelson believed), as from fear of the consequences of a Jacobin triumph. Even the reinforcements gained from the British and Spanish fleets barely enabled Toulon to hold off the Republican forces. The Allies were always in danger; and it is difficult to account for the complacent optimism of such phrases as the following in Mulgrave's private letter of September 15 to Pitt—"I think it a duty of friendship to give you a particular assurance of the confidence I feel of the safety of this place.... If the reinforcements arrive soon, I trust and hope I shall be able to take Marseilles and to keep it." It was not until October 3 that in a private letter to Henry Dundas he breathed a warning as to the unsteadiness of the Spanish and Neapolitan troops; and by a grievous mischance that letter did not reach London until November 14, up to which date ministers believed that all was well at Toulon[1]. Moreover he ended thus his public despatch of October 3, describing the fight on Mt Faron, "I should do injustice were I to particularize any corps or any nation where all were so equally meritorious." It is possible that the Governor of Gibraltar, Sir Robert Boyd, read this despatch without seeing the private warning intended for Dundas. If so, Boyd was naturally reluctant to denude the Rock of troops for the benefit of the presumedly adequate and triumphant garrison of Toulon. Further, the resolve of ministers, on or before October 1,

---

[1] *Dropmore P.*, ii, 445, 464, 471. The date of the letter last referred to should be "November 23," the date of Mulgrave's arrival in London.

to divert part of that garrison to the West Indies was obviously due to the roseate reports early sent off by Mulgrave, which are ultimately accountable for the exasperating muddles that followed. Ministers erred in diffusing their efforts so widely; but he is far more open to censure for misinforming them at first as to the immense difficulties of the defence of Toulon. Fate willed that the first commander at Toulon should be one whose optimism lulled ministers into undue confidence until it was too late to send out succours; and that the second and third commanders should take up the burden when the situation had been compromised by the undue optimism of their predecessor, the bad faith of Austria, and the untrustworthiness of the Spanish and Neapolitan contingents.

Praise has rightly been accorded to Bonaparte for discerning the great importance of the heights of la Grasse; but the foregoing narrative proves that, very early in the defence, Hood and Mulgrave had noted that same fact and that lack of troops alone hindered the formation of a post there. It was Hood, who, on September 20, first warned Mulgrave as to the urgent need of occupying them, otherwise the fleet might have to sail away. That warning constitutes the first written evidence as to the peculiar functions of the combined fleet in the defence. The three first days of Bonaparte's artillery fire endangered the fleet and opened up the question whether it must not weigh anchor. In that case Toulon was untenable.

Yet the presence of the fleet curiously complicated the problem of defence, for it compelled the Allies to defend not only the town but also all the positions commanding both roadsteads. Consequently the defence had to be extended as far as Cape Brun on the east and Fort Mulgrave on the south-west. This extension of the fronts to an enciente of some fifteen miles weakened the defence at any one point. Yet, owing to the configuration of the ground and the vulnerability of the shipping, all the posts were important. None could be neglected without endangering either Toulon or the fleet which covered and fed it. Therein lay the crux of the problem of defence. Its satisfactory solution, as General Dundas saw, required the presence of an army, able not only to drive away first one and then the other of the Republican forces, but to hold them at a distance. The task was by no means impossible during the month of October in view of the marked superiority of the best Allied troops to the raw Republican levies, who gave way at every encounter. But the arrival of reinforcements, both from Lyons and from the armies opposing the somnolent Austro-Sardinian forces, altered the whole situation. Thenceforth a victorious offensive from Toulon as base was impossible.

Even so, however, a stiff and resolute defensive might have worn out the besiegers, provided that reinforcements satisfactory both in quantity and quality reached Toulon in time. O'Hara deemed the presence of 25,000 efficient troops to be necessary even for defence alone[1]. But with them he could surely have crushed one or other of the Republican forces. Even a strict defensive had some prospect of success. Hood's fleet held the sea, and cut off most of the supplies of food so urgently needed by the Republicans, and an adequate patrol either by Spanish vessels or by a flotilla fitted out from the Toulon dockyard might have turned the scale before mid-December. Unfortunately, enough provisions and stores reached the besiegers to enable Bonaparte to make that last effort. It succeeded owing to the poor defence of a few companies of Spaniards at the two crucial points, the right of Fort Mulgrave and the summit of the Pas de la Masque on Mt Faron. Those facts should be noted; for the narrowness of margin in the Jacobinical success ought to dispose of the oft repeated assertion that the defence of Toulon was foredoomed to failure. The presence of 2000 good troops or British seamen would easily have turned the scale on December 17; and in that case the besiegers must have retreated owing to lack of food. The presence of all of Hood's sail-of-the-line at Toulon would also have provided drafts large enough to defend both the positions in question. Or again the arrival in time of the two British regiments from Gibraltar (who were ten days late), or of the 5000 Austrians, who were about to start for Toulon about the end of 1793, would have assured the safety of the place and the discomfiture of the Republicans. In this connection we may note the inner irony of things. The Austrian colonel, belatedly despatched to arrange for

---

[1] H.O. 50, 455, O'Hara to D. Dundas, Nov. 22.

the march of the much-announced 5000, heard of the fall of Toulon at Mantua, where, three years later, Bonaparte was to consummate the ruin of Austria's power in Italy[1]. The withholding of timely support from her Allies at Toulon led to swift and fitting retribution at the hands of the young genius whose early fortunes she had then so signally furthered.

The defence of Toulon is not without interest as an example of amphibious warfare. The position, however, was unfavourable to the joint working of naval and military forces, for, as we have seen, the combined fleet was vulnerable from so many commanding points as to overtax its defenders on shore. Depending absolutely on the fleet for reinforcements, munitions and food, the land forces were by its presence compelled to protect not merely a town but also two extensive roadsteads. This fact was never thoroughly grasped at Whitehall. So late as October 30 the Admiralty received instructions to prepare convoy for the 12th regiment of dragoons, as well as the 40th regiment, about to proceed to Toulon[2],—as though an advance inland were still possible, while, in point of fact, the defence was then confined to a rugged seaboard and rocky peninsula where cavalry were useless. Equally remarkable is it to find Boyd, Governor of Gibraltar, on the report of a Spanish newspaper as to a sortie by 6000 of the Toulon garrison, asserting that as they were able to do that, they needed no reinforcements, and he would not send any[3]. Of the same tenour is a statement of the Austrian Chancellor, Thugut, that there were at Toulon troops "excédant ce que toute place quelconque peut exiger pour sa défense[4]"—an assertion prompted either by ignorance of Toulon topography or by a disloyal desire to evade the despatch of the 5000 Austrians.

The cardinal fact of the situation at Toulon was that, from the time of the advent of Bonaparte, the Republicans dominated the fleet, not it them. Too often it has been assumed that powerful

---

[1] Trevor writing to Grenville from Turin on January 8, 1794, states that Colonel Simshön left Vienna on December 21 to arrange with Trevor details for the march of the 5000 Austrians to the sea for transport to Toulon. S. learnt its fate on arriving at Mantua.

[2] H.O. (Adm. Medit.), 28, vol. 12.

[3] Gen. Dundas's letter of November 22 (H.O. Mil. Medit. 1793).

[4] Vivenot, *Quellen zur Geschichte der deutschen Kaiserpolitik Oesterreichs*, III, 385.

broadsides can overbear shore batteries; and doubtless this is true in cases where the broadsides are brought to bear at close range on equal terms as at Portobello or Acre. But these conditions did not exist at Toulon. There the ships' guns were ineffective, partly because shallow water hindered their near approach to the only shore which was nearly level with them.

Indeed, a British fleet has never had a more thankless task than at Toulon. The ships told off for cannonading, especially the 'Princess Royal,' were under constant fire to which they could make no adequate reply. The crews were weakened by being sent ashore at every crisis; and some of them helped continuously to man the fortifications. As to the value of this assistance General Dundas bore testimony. On December 21, while in Hières Bay, he wrote to Henry Dundas—

> The general service has been carried out with the most perfect harmony and zeal of the Navy and Army. From our deficiency in artillerymen, many of our batteries were worked by seamen. They in part guarded some of our Posts, and their aid was peculiarly useful in duties of fatigue and labour. In all these we found the influence of the superior activity and exertions of British sailors. It was the constant attention of Lord Hood to relieve our wants and alleviate our difficulties[1].

The panegyric is just, and it disposes of the charge that has been made against Hood as to his "usually contemptuous attitude towards military officers[2]."

Nevertheless the fact remains that the landing of seamen in order to help protect their own ships is not a very effective way of using them. We are brought back to Nelson's criticism, penned on August 20 off Toulon,—"It seems of no use to send a great fleet here without troops to act with them[3]." The Allies of course were to provide the troops; but British seamen had to make up for their deficiencies—a highly undesirable type of amphibious warfare.

That naval co-operation was loyally maintained in spite of exposure, fatigue, annoyance with Allies, and a creeping sense of hopelessness, is a fine tribute to Lord Hood and his officers and

---

[1] H.O. 50, 456.
[2] Fortescue, IV, Pt. I, 173. I dissent from the judgment there given as to Hood's conduct of the defence.   [3] Nicolas, I, 320.

men. They and the British and Sardinian troops bore the brunt
of the defence. Without Hood's indomitable spirit Toulon could
not have been held for a month. His optimism during the first
weeks was due mainly to the reports of Mulgrave. His obsession
by this manliest of defects exposed him to sharp censure; and it
may be granted that he should have prepared more systematically
for the eventuality of evacuation. Even on December 17 he opposed that step, probably from a feeling that he was bound in
honour to protect to the uttermost the city and population confided to his charge. The statement of a Spanish naval historian[1],
that Hood had throughout endeavoured to secure the French
arsenal ships, and stores, and was prevented only by the action
of the Spaniards, is at variance with the evidence. If Hood had
been so intent on the destruction or withdrawal of the French
fleet he would not have met with opposition from the Spaniards,
whose Government during the month of October favoured that
step; and, as has been seen, Langara incautiously divulged the
secret. Also Sir Sidney Smith's account of his attempt to burn
the French fleet on December 18, represents it as planned somewhat hurriedly, almost as an afterthought, and Revel's assertion,
that at the final council of war Hood alone opposed the evacuation, refutes the slander that he all along thought mainly of destroying or withdrawing the French fleet. Had all the Allies
shared his high resolve to hold Toulon, it would have been held.
Finally, in view of the small number of British ships present at
Toulon on December 17–19, it reflects great credit on him and
his officers that they brought off on those ships the British, Sardinian, and part of the Neapolitan forces, together with a large
number of refugees. The reproaches of certain French writers as
to the small number of Royalists rescued by Hood's ships are
unfounded.

Viewed from a more general standpoint, the defence and siege
of Toulon in 1793 are typical instances of the manifestation of
the old spirit and the new then meeting in death grapple. Out-
wardly, events betokened an easy victory for *l'ancien régime*; but
the incurable jealousies and senile lethargy of the old monarchies
hindered all effective use of that unexampled occasion, while the

[1] Duro, *Armada española*, VIII, 42.

nascent forces of democracy and nationality, embattled on the side of the Republic, drew strength out of the disasters of August 1793 and metamorphosed them into the triumphs of December. A survey of the influences that told against the Allies should not overlook the moral influences which mysteriously energized the Republicans so soon as their domestic enemies summoned in the foreigner. Thenceforth a blight descended on French Royalism, as appears from O'Hara's letter of November 13:

> The people of this country [so he wrote at Toulon to Dundas], from the first arrival of the English, have never taken any active part in supporting the common cause. A want of energy pervades the whole. They seem solely to depend on the combined forces for their defence, and on their humanity for their subsistence; and I am told that this apathy extends to the whole of this and the neighbouring provinces[1].

O'Hara here touched the weak spot of the Toulon enterprise. While Pitt and his colleagues hopefully pictured it as inaugurating a great Royalist movement that would sweep northwards and effect the relief of Lyons and the overthrow of the Parisian despots, in reality it paralysed the Royalists and nerved the Jacobins to more desperate exertions. As had been truly foretold by Bonaparte in his first political pamphlet, *le Souper de Beaucaire*, the calling in of a foreign fleet damned the party which resorted to that unpatriotic expedient. "If you do that" (he says in effect to *le Marseillais*), "you will in a week have sixty thousand patriots ranged against you." The forecast proclaimed his political sagacity. No event of that age tended so much to rally the nation to the Jacobins. Thenceforth they were fired with the resolve to recover a great dockyard handed over by the Royalists to the lords of the sea. It was these imponderables, no less than the perfidy at Berlin and the mistakes at Gibraltar, Whitehall, Madrid and Vienna, which lost Toulon.

Probably no event of that age was more fruitful in consequences. The mutual confidence of the Allies suffered a shock from which it never fully recovered. Thenceforth Spain cherished for the British an incurable distrust, which was deepened when their next

---

[1] H.O. 50, 455. So too Wickham in 1795—"Since the affair of Toulon they [the Provençaux] have imbibed the most violent hatred against all foreigners" (*Corresp. of W. Wickham*, I, 93).

move proved to be against Corsica. The French Royalists harboured hard thoughts against us for alleged heedlessness during the evacuation; and this was but natural when the triumphant Jacobins deluged Toulon with blood. Jacobinical energy, however, reconstructed the French fleet with phenomenal speed. Ten months later, Nelson wrote "The French have put together a fleet at Toulon, which could hardly be credited[1]." The challenge to French pride evoked a will to conquer both by land and sea; and from Toulon went forth both the army that overran North Italy and the armada designed for the conquest of the East. Neither of these efforts could have been put forth had the Allies utilized with even moderate energy the opportunity placed in their hands at the end of August 1793.

[1] Nicolas, I, 500.

APPENDICES

APPENDIX A

ADMIRALTY INSTRUCTIONS TO V.-ADM. LORD HOOD

N.B. All orders are to Hood, unless otherwise specified. The less important orders are here summarized. The date of the year 1793 is omitted. The following abbreviations are used:

> V. Adm. = Vice-Admiral.
> R. Adm. = Rear-Admiral.
> Y. Lp. = Your Lordship.
> Y. Ex. = Your Excellency.

Secret. 24 March.

Y. Lp. is hereby directed to order R. Adm. Gell to take under his command H.M.'s ships named in the margin[1], and to accompany the 'Powerful' with the East India Company's ships under her convoy 200 leagues to Westward of the Lizard when he is to direct the Capt. of the 'Boyne' to put himself under the command of the Capt. of the 'Powerful'...he is then to proceed with the rest of the ships under his command off the Azores and to cruise...for the protection of the Trade...and the annoyance of the enemy...Y. Lp. will instruct the R. Adm. to continue in that service until the 25th of next month, when...the R. Adm. is to proceed with the 'St George,' 'Egmont,' 'Leda,' and 'L'Aigle' to Gibraltar Bay where he is to complete their water and provisions without loss of time and keep himself and them in constant readiness for sea, until he sees or hears from Y. Lp. unless he should be otherwise directed by R. Adm. Goodall.

Secret. 5 April.

...Y. Lp. is directed to give orders to V. Adm. Cosby to put to sea (on the 10th inst.) with H.M.'s ships named in the margin[2] and give protection to the Trade bound to the coasts of Spain and Portugal as far as his way and theirs may lie together, and to the West India Trade 200 leagues to the Westward of the Lizard, when he is to proceed to Cape Finisterre to cruize from thence 40 or 50 leagues N.W. for ten days and then make the best of his way off Cape Spartel and cruize between that and Cape Trafalgar from 10 to 15 leagues from the land until the 15th of next month when he is to

---

[1] 'St George,' 'Boyne,' 'Ganges,' 'Edgar,' 'Egmont,' 'Phaeton,' 'Leda,' 'L'Aigle.'
[2] 'Windsor Castle,' 'Princess Royal,' 'Alcide,' 'Illustrious,' 'Terrible.'

repair to the Bay of Gibraltar where he is to use his best diligence in completing the watering and provisions (as far as the victualling stores there will permit) of the ships under his command, and to wait until he sees or hears from Y. Lp., taking under his orders R. Adms. Goodall and Gell with such of H.M.'s ships and vessels as he finds or may arrive at Gibraltar and holding the whole in constant readiness for the sea.

On April 23 to take under his command 'Berwick' (Sir John Collins), 'Mermaid' (Mr Trigge), 'Castor' (Thos.Troubridge), 'Nemesis' (Jno. Woodley), 'Hind' (Hon. A. F. Cochrane), 'Tartar' (Alex. Guyot), 'Amphitrite' (Jas. Dickinson); on April 25 to take 'Captain' (Capt. Reeve); on April 30 frigate 'Meleager' (Capt. Tyler); on May 1 sloop 'Tisiphone' (Capt. Hunt—later, B. Martin).

23 April.

To take the ships named under his command and employ them as he shall judge best for H.M.'s service. 'Mermaid,' 'Castor,' fifth rates. 'Nemesis,' 'Hind,' 'Amphitrite,' 'Tartar,' sixth rates.

4 May.

To repair to Portsmouth and hoist his flag on the 'Victory,' and remain there until further order.

Secret. 8 May.

He will order V. Adm. Hotham with the ships in the margin[1] to proceed directly off Ushant in order to protect a convoy expected from Gibraltar under H.M.S. 'Assistance,' and, having seen it safely into the English Channel, to return off the Lizard and await Y. Lp. unless he receives further orders.

18 May.

Upon all occasions to give any ships belonging to the States Gen. of the United Provinces the same protection and assistance as would be afforded by him to the ships of H.M.'s subjects under similar circumstances. To take under his protection the trading vessels belonging to Spain, Portugal and Prussia, which may happen to fall in his course, and to take such measures for their security as are not inconsistent with H.M.'s service.

Secret. 18 May.

Whereas the King has thought fit to order a powerful fleet to be employed in the Mediterranean for the purpose of affording effectual protection to the commerce of H.M.'s subjects in those seas, as well as of attempting some decisive Blow against the Naval Power of

[1] 'Britannia,' 'Courageux,' 'Fortitude,' 'Colossus,' 'Agamemnon,' 'Juno,' 'Meleager.'

France; and whereas by our commission bearing date the 13th of March last Y. Lp. was appointed commander in chief of H.M.'s ships and vessels employed and to be employed in the Mediterranean, and the V. Adms. Hotham and Cosby, R. Adm. Gell and a squadron of H.M.'s ships and vessels have been since put under your command and Y. Lp. has, pursuant to our orders, sent Detachments of the said squadron upon particular services, under the separate commands of those officers, with directions to V. Adm. Cosby and R. Adm. Gell to repair afterwards with part of those under their respective commands to Gibraltar, and to V. Adm. Hotham to return with those under his command off the Lizard and remain there until he shall be joined by you; and whereas we intend that Y. Lp. shall proceed forthwith to Gibraltar with the remainder of your squadron, you are hereby required and directed to put to sea, the first opportunity of wind and weather, taking under your convoy such storeships, victuallers and Trade bound to Gibraltar and the Mediterranean as may be at Spithead ready to accompany you, and then proceed down Channel, and, having joined V. Adm. Hotham with the ships under his orders, make the best of your way, consistent with the security of the said storeships, victuallers and Trade, to Gibraltar.

On your arrival there Y. Lp. will take under your command R. Adm. Goodall, who is directed to obey your orders, and H.M.'s ships and vessels already on the Mediterranean station, and, having assembled your Fleet, will lose no time in obtaining the best Intelligence of the force and destination of the enemy and use your best endeavours to seek the French Fleet and to bring it to action.

But in case, as is most probable, it should return to Toulon, Y. Lp. will then take such a station and for such time and in such manner as circumstances shall point out to you to be advisable, in order to enable you to watch the motions of the French Fleet and to collect with the aid of the frigates etc. under your command the numerous Trade of H.M.'s subjects from the various Ports of the Mediterranean and to afford effectual protection to its assembling in some place of safety, where it should remain till you receive further instructions from us, as to what convoy will be sent from hence to receive it at Gibraltar; whether any part of the force under your command should be detached with it, or whether yourself with the whole or principal part of your Fleet will be to escort it to England, and which decision must depend very much on the destination and strength of the Western squadron and on the knowledge of the operations in the Mediterranean, in which you may be eventually engaged, and their probable duration.

And whereas the Rt. Hon. Henry Dundas, one of H.M.'s principal Secs. of State, hath acquainted us by his letter of this date that H.M. has given directions to His Ambassadors at the Courts of Spain,

Portugal, Naples and Sardinia to enter into negotiations for the purpose of establishing a concert between H.M. and the said Courts as to the most effectual means to be taken in order to act against the common enemy, and hath signified to us H.M.'s pleasure as to the necessary instructions to be given in the meantime to Y. Lp. upon that subject, We do, in pursuance of H.M.'s said pleasure, hereby further require and direct you to cooperate as far as circumstances may permit with the Commanders of the Fleets and Armies of the Powers above mentioned, in carrying into effect such measures as (in the interval of the final establishment of such concert) may suggest themselves on the spot to Y. Lp. and the Commanders of the said Fleets and Armies who will no doubt be particularly instructed to communicate with you as to the most effectual means of acting against the common enemy. And Y. Lp. will not fail to avail yourself of every favourable occasion of opening an intimate and confidential intercourse with them respecting the several operations which may present themselves in the course of the ensuing campaign; as well as to use every means in your power of cultivating the utmost harmony and good understanding between you and the governors, officers etc. of the Powers above mentioned; and you will neglect no opportunity not only of impressing on the States bordering on the Mediterranean an Idea of the strength and Power of Great Britain, but also of manifesting (in your conduct) H.M.'s earnest desire of affording protection and support to all lawful and established authority, and of maintaining inviolate the rights of sovereign and independent Nations against the dangers with which they are threatened on the part of France; and you will of course consider yourself as at liberty to give the aid and assistance of the Fleet under your command in defending the Coasts and Territories of H.M.'s Allies and of the States in amity with H.M., against any attacks with which they may be threatened, as well as in protecting and covering any attacks to be made (against the common enemy) in the prosecution of which your cooperation may be desired, bearing always in mind that the leading object of your Instructions is to give Battle to the Fleet of France and to secure to H.M.'s subjects and those of His Allies the free and uninterrupted navigation of the Mediterranean.

Y. Lp. (after having fulfilled the more immediate object of your instructions) will hold yourself and the Fleet under your command in constant readiness either to return to England with the Trade which you shall have assembled, or to undertake such operations as H.M. shall hereafter direct in consequence of the concert and cooperation to be established between H.M. and the Courts of Spain, Portugal, Naples and Sardinia as above mentioned, unless you should be already engaged therein, in obedience to the general instructions already given to that effect.

If, on your arrival at Gibraltar, you shall find any homeward bound

Trade assembled to a considerable amount, Y. Lp. will immediately or as soon afterwards as you shall find it expedient, appoint one of the 64 gun ships or any of the others you shall judge proper of the Fleet under your command, to convoy such Trade to England, giving us the earliest notice of the time fixed for their departure and of the ship or ships so appointed by Y. Lp. and directing the commanding officer of the convoy to use his best endeavours to see the Trade in safety to the Downes or as far as his way and theirs shall lie together and to remain there until further order, sending to our secretary an account of his arrival and proceedings.

(Sent to Lord Hood at Spithead by a messenger on the 20th at 5 p.m.)

Separate. 18 May.

In pursuance of the King's pleasure signified to us by the Rt. Hon. Henry Dundas, one of H.M.'s principal Secs. of State, in his separate letter of this date, Y. Lp. is hereby required and directed to despatch, as soon as possible after your arrival in the Mediterranean, an officer to Genoa...in order that Y. Lp. may be able to judge when and how far it will be in your power consistently with the other important objects of your instructions, to take measures for facilitating or assisting in such operations. And, in that case, you will lose no opportunity of giving all the aid and assistance which circumstances may render practicable.

To R. Adm. Goodall, Gibraltar. Secret. 18 May.

To put himself under the command of Lord Hood.

Secret. 20 May.

So soon as seven of the line of battle ships under Y. Lp.'s command at Spithead shall be in all respects ready, Y. Lp. is hereby required and directed (notwithstanding anything to the contrary in your former instructions) to put to sea; leaving orders for the other two to follow you; and having joined V. Adm. Hotham you will detach two sail of the line and two frigates or such force as you shall judge necessary with the convoy to Gibraltar, and the 'Phaeton' and 'Kingfisher' with that to Spain and Portugal; and you will then cruize off Ushant with the remainder until the homeward bound Trade and convoy of the 'Assistance' shall have passed in safety into the Channel and Y. Lp. will then stretch into the Bay in order to intercept any French ships that may be cruizing there. At the same time you will endeavour to regulate your conduct according to circumstances so as, if possible, not to delay your arrival at Gibraltar (for the purpose of carrying into execution our secret instructions of the 18th inst.) beyond the time when it may be probable that the convoy detached by Y. Lp. may be likely to reach Gibraltar.

Secret. 24 August.

(Terms of the treaty with Sardinia regarding the employment of 6000 troops and warships of that Power in the Mediterranean.)

Y. Lp. is required and directed to make the necessary requisition for the said ships and vessels and land forces when you shall see occasion for them and to employ the same as shall be judged most advisable in cooperating with the squadron under your command in any operations which you may judge it expedient to undertake for the recovery of Nice or for the relief of Corsica or in any other way Y. Lp. may think most conducive to H.M.'s service, acting either separately or in conjunction with any of the Powers in the Mediterranean in amity with Great Britain or disposed to take part in the common cause against France.

Secret. 24 Sept.

To order R. Adm. Gell to proceed with all possible speed to Gibraltar in the 'St George,' together with two 74's and a frigate, to follow the orders he will receive there.

26 Sept.

Approbation of his services first in the blockade and then in the occupation of Toulon. He is to convey to Capt. Elphinstone and the troops serving under him H.M.'s satisfaction with their exertions in his service.

Secret. 28 Sept.

To send the 'Leviathan' to Gibraltar in addition to the ships mentioned in the instructions of the 24th inst.

Secret. 29 Sept.

Notwithstanding order of 24th inst. he need not send a frigate to Gibraltar with R. Adm. Gell, if it is not convenient.

Secret. 1 October.

To remove the soldiers of the 30th Regt. serving as marines, as part of the complement of the 'Princess Royal,' 'Robust' and 'Terrible,' into the 'St George' and other ships to go to Gibraltar with R. Adm. Gell, and to supply their places with soldiers or marines serving on board the ships he may send with Gell. To cause the party of the 30th Regt. serving on board the 'Alcide' in lieu of marines, to be removed into the 'Leviathan,' and the party of the 11th Regt. serving in the 'Leviathan' to be transferred to the 'Alcide.'

To R. Adm. Gell.   Secret. 15 Oct.

To proceed at once to Barbadoes and there put himself under the command of V. Adm. Sir John Jervis.

To R. Adm. Gell.   Secret. 15 November.

Notwithstanding the secret order of the 15th ult. he is to return with all possible despatch and rejoin Adm. Lord Hood with the 'St George' and the two 74's, and to follow H. Lp.'s orders again for his further proceedings.

APPENDIX B[1]

LORD HOOD'S JOURNAL

May 25. 'Britannia,' 'Courageux,' 'Colossus,' 'Fortitude,' 'Agamemnon,' 'Lowestoft,' and 'Meleager' joined company.

June 20. 'Bulldog' joined company. Entered Gibraltar Bay.

July 21–23. Strong gales.

,, 24. 28 sail of the Fleet in company.

Aug. 2. 'Romulus' joined Fleet.

,, 9. Parted company 'Robust,' 'Colossus,' 'Agamemnon,' 'Romulus.'

,, 15. 1.28 p.m. Parted company 'Meleager' and 'Conflagration.'
4 p.m. Parted co. 'Windsor Castle,' 'Terrible,' 'Bedford,'
'Lowestoft,' 'Vulcan.'

,, 16. 5.30 p.m. Strange fleet sighted.

,, 21. 'Robust,' 'Colossus,' 'Agamemnon,' 'Mermaid,' 'Romney'
joined company.

,, 25. 5 p.m. Boat with flag of truce from Toulon came on board.

,, 26. 6 p.m. Flag of truce from Toulon.

,, 28. 'Romulus,' 'Nemesis,' 'Vulcan,' joined co.
5 a.m. Spanish fleet sighted to West.
9 a.m. 'Egmont,' 'Robust,' 'Courageux,' 'Colossus,' 'Meleager,' 'Tartar' stood in to land some troops to East of
Toulon.
9.15 a.m. Fort of La Malgue opened in view to the
'Victory.' Hoisted all the boats out and hove to. Observed
the blue flag flying at the Fort and at the Round Tower,
being the Signal to intimate their being ready to admit our
troops.

Sept. 2. Arrived four Spanish ships of the line and a frigate.

,, 12. Lt. Inman with 30 men took charge of 'Aurora,' French
frigate.

,, 18. 4 a.m. Cannonade between 'Aurora' and forts ashore.
Floating battery No. 1 firing at the same time.

,, 19. 5.55 p.m. Brisk cannonade from 'St George,' 'Aurora' and
Floating battery. Placed another floating battery in N.W.
Arm, no. 3.

,, 20. 11 a.m. Floating Battery No. 1 hauled off, having received
much damage.

[1] The Journal is imperfect: *e.g.* Hood does not note the arrival of the
'Terrible' and 'Iris' with troops on Oct. 27, though he records that of
'Egmont' on Oct. 28.

Sept. 21. 2 p.m. Cannonade still in N.W. Arm.

,, 24. Cannonade by our mortar and gunboats in N.W. Arm.

,, 27. 11 p.m. Ships in N.W. Arm began to fire on enemy.

,, 28. 5 p.m. A Neapolitan squadron arrived.

,, 29. 11 a.m. Arrived two Spanish mortar boats.

Oct. 6. 8 p.m. Anchored a Spanish frigate and a Neapolitan sloop with several Neapolitan vessels with troops.

,, 12. 10.30 a.m. 'Courageux' went into Inner Road.

,, 13. Arrived 'La Modeste' and two gunboats.

,, 17. 8 p.m. Several launches taking troops from Toulon to Cape Cepet.

8 a.m. Arrived Sardinian frigate and two vessels with Piedmontese troops.

,, 18. 5 p.m. Heavy fire began from Haut. de Grasse and ships in N.W. Arm.

,, 20. Cannonading in N.W. Arm.

,, 28. 4 p.m. Arrived 'Egmont' with troops.

Nov. 3. p.m. Firing in N.W. Arm and from Hauteur de Grasse.

,, 5. 3 p.m. Heavy cannonading from 'Aurora' and gunboats in S.W. Arm.

,, 13. 8 a.m. Came out of Harbour and anchored the 'Commerce de Marseilles.'

,, 14. 4.30 p.m. Sent four 24 prs. in French launch to Fort Mulgrave.

,, 15. 9 a.m. Sent to Fort Mulgrave two 24 prs. with 180 shot.

Dec. 5. 4.30 p.m. Arrived Neapolitan ship of line and a frigate with troops.

,, 17. 3.10 a.m. Made signal for all boats of fleet to disembark troops.

4 a.m. Officer came on board to report taking of Fort Mulgrave.

10 a.m. 'Pompey,' 'Commerce de Marseilles' with the different gun and mortar boats firing at enemy on Fort Mulgrave.

Noon. Came out of Inner Harbour and anchored H.M.S. 'Terrible,' 'Robust' and 'Courageux.'

,, 18. 8 a.m. Receiving French refugee families.

,, 19. 9 p.m. Received on board number of troops and baggage.

10 p.m. Sent all our boats to assist in embarking troops from the shore.

4.30 a.m. Weighed and made sail as did all the fleet out of Toulon Harbour. The fire still continuing.

APPENDIX C

LOGS OF THE 'VICTORY,' 'BRITANNIA,' 'PRINCESS ROYAL,' 'ST GEORGE,' 'WINDSOR CASTLE'

[The logs of most of the ships are very meagre. The following are the best. Unimportant details are omitted.]

'VICTORY' (Log of Captain J. Knight).

May 23. Started from Spithead in company with the 'Robust,' 'Bedford,' 'Berwick,' 'Captain,' 'Leviathan,' 'Ardent,' 'St Albans,' 'Camel,' 'Dolphin,' 'Phaeton,' 'La Aimable,' 'Tartar,' 'Amphitrite,' 'Castor,' 'Vulcan,' 'Tisiphone,' 'Conflagration,' and a convoy of East Indiamen.

June 20. Arrived Gibraltar. Left 28 June.

July 20. French prize sent into Toulon with flag of truce.

Aug. 23. French Carteel from Marseilles joined fleet.

,,   24. Flag of truce sent into Toulon; returned 25th.

,,   28. Troops landed from fleet. Saw 18 sail of Spanish men of war W.S.W. Observed several French men of war go into inner Harbour of Toulon.

,,   29. Entered Toulon.

Sept. 1. The French men of war stripping.

,,   17. Three French line ships sailed with their guns out, full of men, a fourth ran on shore. Spanish ship of the line sailed with them.

,,   18. Saw cannonade on N.W. Arm between 'Aurora' and enemy on shore.

,,   19. French ship aground on 17th got off and sailed. Brisk cannonade on N.W. arm. Placed another floating battery on N.W. arm.

,,   20. Brisk cannonade on N.W. arm. At 11 no. 1 floating battery hauled off having received much damage.

,,   21. At 11 sent boats to convoy troops from Toulon to N.W. shore. At 9 a.m. floating battery no. 3 sunk by enemy in N.W. arm.

,,   22. Our people employed clearing and fortifying heights called the New Post[1].

,,   27. 11 a.m. Ships began to fire on enemy. 'Bedford' and 'Leviathan' arrived with troops.

,,   28. Neapolitan squadron arrived with troops.

[1] Fort Mulgrave.

Oct. 1. Enemy took possession of heights and Eastern position over Toulon. At 7 Adm. Gell and squadron sailed. At 10 combined troops move against the enemy. French men of war hoisted white flags and saluted. At 11.30 saw our troops on the heights.

„ 2. 3.30 p.m. Enemy retreated from Eastern Post and our troops took possession.

„ 6. Several Neapolitan transports arrived with troops.

„ 13. Arrival of 'Modeste' and two gunboats, prizes to Adm. Gell. Ships and gunboats firing at the enemy.

„ 27. Arrival of H.M.S. 'Terrible' and 'Iris' with troops.

„ 28. 'Egmont' arrives with troops. Salute to Gen. O'Hara on going ashore.

„ 29. Arrival of Spanish line ship and two frigates with troops.

Nov. 15. Salute to Sir G. Elliot on coming aboard. Sent two 24 pounders to Fort Mulgrave.

Dec. 5. Arrival of Neapolitan ships with troops.

„ 17. At 5 a.m. officer came on board to report that the enemy had taken Fort Mulgrave. 'Commerce de Marseille,' 'Pompey' and different gunboats firing at enemy at Fort Mulgrave. Came out of inner and anchored in outer road H.M. Ships 'Terrible,' 'Robust' and 'Courageux.'

„ 18. Weighed and warped further out. At 8 p.m. anchored. All employed receiving French refugee men, women and children. At 10 moved farther out as did the whole fleet.

„ 19. At 9 p.m. observed a great fire, supposed to be the ships and Arsenal. Sent all boats to assist embarking troops. Received some on board. Weighed and made sail with all the fleet out of Toulon Harbour. At noon anchored in Hières Bay.

„ 21. Sailed from hence the Spanish fleet.

'BRITANNIA' (Log of Captain J. Holloway).

May 7 (Tuesday). V. Adm. Hood hoisted his flag: saluted the 'Victory' with three cheers.

„ 12. 3 p.m. Made signal for white squadron to weigh anchor; 'Britannia,' 'Courageux,' 'Fortitude,' 'Agamemnon,' 'Colossus,' 'Lowestoft,' 'Meleager.'

June 28. Working out of Gibraltar Bay with the squadron and convoy. At 7 the 'St Albans,' 'Bulldog' and convoy parted company.

Aug. 23. (Cape Cicie N.E. by N. 3 or 4 leagues.) 14 sail of line, 2 frigates and 1 fireship in company.

„ 27. Joined the fleet the 'Windsor Castle,' 'Bedford,' 'Terrible,' 'Vulcan' and Sardinian frigate.

„ 28. Sent our two companies of the 69th Regt. on 'Courageux' to be landed at Toulon. The 'Colossus,' 'Egmont,' 'Robust' and 'Courageux,' 'Meleager' and 'Tartar' to anchor immediately.

Aug. 29. At noon anchored in Outer Road, Toulon. P.M. sent 50 men, 1 lieut. and 2 midshipmen on the 'Meleager' to be landed at Toulon.

Oct. 1. Sailed R. Adm. Gell in 'St George' with 'Bedford,' 'Captain,' 'Tartar,' 'Vulcan,' 'Conflagration,' 'L'Éclair,' 'Speedy' and 'Alert,' a Spanish Admiral with two sail of line and one French ship of the line.

,, 13. The gunboats in the S.W. arm firing at a new work of the enemy's.

,, 14. A party round Cape Sepet demolishing the batteries.

,, 17. Arrived a Sardinian frigate and convoy with troops: sailed the 'Windsor Castle' with a Neapolitan ship of the line, 4 frigates and a convoy.

,, 21. Arrived the 'Captain' with a French frigate under English colours, also a Spanish three-decker and one two-decker.

,, 27. Arrived the 'Terrible,' 'Iris' with troops from Gibraltar.

,, 28. Arrived the 'Egmont.'

Nov. 1. Court martial on Capt. Lumsdaine of the 'Iris,' for disobeying the orders of the commr.-in-chief; who was acquitted.

,, 6. Sailed three Spanish ships of the line.

,, 11. Arrived 'Leviathan,' 'Fortitude,' a corvette under Eng. colours, 'La Perle,' and two merchantmen, the 'Tartar' and 'Scout' (brig).

,, 22. Arrived several merchantmen.

Dec. 10. Arrived two Span. sail of line and a frigate.

,, 11. Arrived 'Romulus,' 'Sincere' and 'Tartar.'

,, 14. Sailed 'Diadem' and 'Tartar.'

,, 17. No. 46, a.m. at 2 for all boats, at do. Ft. Mulgrave attacked, and about 4 the firing ceased, the enemy having drove our troops from the post. At $\frac{1}{2}$ p. 11 the boats of the fleet carrying the troops from Hauteur de Grasse, having evacuated the post.

,, 18 (calm, variable). Warped a mile further out: the fleets employed warping into the Outer Road: the enemy in possession of many of the outposts.

,, 19. The boats of the fleets embarking the army from La Malgue: bore up for Hières Road.

,, 21. Sailed from Hières Road the Spanish fleet and 'Romulus.'

'PRINCESS ROYAL' (Log of Captain J. C. Purvis).

May 15. Gibraltar Bay. Found riding 'St George,' 'Alcide,' 'Egmont,' 'Illustrious,' 'Aquilon' and 'Bulldog,' 'Terrible.'

Aug. 25. Admiral hoisted the Comet, indicating that the Fleet were not to be governed by his example, when he stood close into the entrance of Toulon; boats passing with flags of truce to and from the Harbour. The 'Conflagration' plying close in with a flag of truce.

Aug. 27. Joined the Fleet V. Adm. Cosby in 'Windsor Castle,' with 'Terrible,' 'Bedford,' 'Vulcan,' from Genoa.

,, 28. Order to send all troops on board the 'Robust' as soon as possible. A Spanish fleet of 17 sail of the line and one frigate to windward at 7.30. At 9 the following ships stood into Toulon, having all the troops on board from the fleet, 'Egmont,' 'Robust,' 'Colossus,' 'Courageux,' 'Meleager' and 'Tartar.' Sent a Lieut. with two midshipmen and 45 men to take on them the business of gunners in the forts. At 11.30 all the troops landed without any opposition, and marched up to Fort de la Malgue, which was delivered up to them.

,, 29. On the troops entering Fort La Malgue the French National colours were hoisted, as they were at all the French forts. The ships in the Outer Road getting into the Inner one as fast as possible to make room for the English ships.

,, 30. Sent another party on shore consisting of a Lieut. midshipman and 30 seamen, the enemy having advanced and a large party of the troops having gone out against them from Fort La Malgue.

Sept. 1. The officer, midshipman and 30 men returned from the Fort. They brought an account of a large party of our troops had marched out in the evening and attacked a considerable body of the enemy to the Westward; that we had killed and wounded many of them, and taken their colours and two field pieces; but that we lost Capt. Douglas, Town Major of Gibraltar, who was shot thro' the body, and several of the men wounded. A.M. I was sent to the South side of Cape Sepet to dismount some guns there. Took a party with a Lieut. and midshipman and spiked up and threw down the Rocks nine cannon, 36 pounders, and a mortar of 13 in.

,, 7. In the night an advanced post to Westward was attacked by the enemy, by which we had near 100 men killed and wounded, mostly Spaniards. The enemy lost many but the number not known.

,, 11. Sent 36 labourers with a midshipman to work at Fort Malbosquet.

,, 14. Sent two midshipmen and 30 seamen to man a large Pontoon mounting four 24 pounders. I was sent to place and move another of the same kind to command the isthmus leading to Sepet.

,, 19. Enemy opened some other two gun Batterys and we armed another large pontoon to oppose them.

Sept. 20. This day has been the warmest the pontoons have had, the enemy firing red hot shot.

,,   21. Sent launch and two cutters to assist in carrying troops from the town to the land on the West end of the Harbour (Hauteur de Grasse) on the height of which they took post and in the morning sent a midshipman and a party of 33 labourers to assist in throwing up trenches.

,,   22. 5.30. Signal for all launches to repair to Western shore ready to take off the troops if they should be obliged to embark, the enemy having attacked them. At 7 a.m. transporting cannon and the crew assisting in getting them up the height where the troops are posted.

,,   23. 1 p.m. Sent midshipman with 20 men to assist in throwing up works round the height where the troops are posted.

,,   24. Hauled ship across the Harbour to have her broadside the enemy and cleared ship for action. Ships and pontoons in this quarter cannonade the town La Seyne all night.

,,   25. At 4 p.m. the four gun Battery began firing. Do. began our lower deck guns at them assisted by a Spanish line of battle ship. The French frigate 'Aurora' with Englishmen on board and two armed pontoons, at 5.30 ceased firing. At 8 a.m. began firing again on battery, occasionally leaving off, supposing the battery silenced; but on firing again we did the same on them and continued firing at intervals till noon. The Spanish ship having received a shot or two hauled off and left us.

,,   26. At 3 p.m. having driven the enemy from the Battery, ceased firing. In the night fired into the town La Seyne and threw several shells by way of keeping up the alarm and harassing the enemy, though much mischief was done to the poor inhabitants.

,,   27. Fired a great many of the lower deck guns at the Battery.

,,   28. Neapolitan troops arrive.

,,   29. Enemy employed making a new Battery between the windmills on the heights to windward of the Hauteur de Grasse.

,,   30. 3 p.m. Hove in the springs and brought guns to bear on the enemy's Battery. At 4 on the enemy's firing at us we began at them and continued at intervals till the day closed in. The 'Aurora' having received several shot in her hull was ordered off; remains now with us a French 74, 'Le Puissant,' a bomb frigate and two armed pontoons.

Oct.   2. Action on Faron. All the action and the advance towards it was in full view of the fleet, but more particularly so from us who enjoyed the sight of a glorious achievement gained with little loss and which displayed an infinite deal of judgment and valour in the officers and men who were concerned in it. A.M. fired some of the lower deck guns at the four gun Battery.

Oct. 6. Enemy opened a two gun battery close to that of four guns.

,, 9. At 9 commenced firing at the enemy's Batterys and continued at intervals till 11.

,, 11. Enemy began throwing shell at us, some of which came very near the ship.

,, 12. 1 p.m. Enemy began to fire at us, began our lower deck guns at them and continued firing at intervals till 5.30 when all firing ceased.

,, 13. 1 p.m. On enemy firing from their batteries both shot and shell opened our fire at them and continued at intervals till 5.30. One of the shells struck the ship just below the water line, but did no mischief. Many others fell near us all round. Some of the running rigging was cut by the shot. At 8.30 a.m. began our fire on the enemy as before and continued at intervals all day.

,, 14. 5 p.m. Ceased firing; at noon began firing on enemy.

,, 15. At 6 ceased firing. Received a large shot just abaft the larboard cathead.

,, 16. At 10 a.m. began firing at the enemy as usual.

,, 18. At 4 p.m. on the enemy firing on us opened ours on them and continued at intervals till 5.30.

,, 19. 5.30 p.m. Enemy began their fire at us both with shot and shells being a very fine moonlight evening. Immediately returned their fire from our lower deck guns till 7 when we ceased firing; the enemy continuing throwing shells, some of which came near us, and one broke nearly over our heads but did no mischief. The Spanish bomb vessel throwing shells at the Battery till nearly 11 o'clock.

,, 20. 5 p.m. Enemy began firing; we returned their fire; continued till 6 o'clock when we ceased.

,, 23. At 4 p.m. the enemy firing on us, opened our fire on them, one of the lower deck guns burst, four men killed, two lieutenants and 29 men wounded, many of them very badly.

,, 26. Anniversary of King's Accession. Fired salute of 19 guns, all on starboard side with shot at the enemy at 1 p.m. which brought on a return from them and was continued till 4 by us, when we ceased. Received several of the enemy's shot, some of which weighed 44 pounds.

,, 27. Exchanging fire 3 to 5 p.m.

Nov. 2. At 12.30 the Battery began firing at us and continued till 4 in the morning but in consequence of our veering away none of their shot struck us though they came very near us.

,, 3. 1 p.m. Returned enemy's fire and soon after a red hot shot came in at one of the lower deck ports, disabled the gun by knocking off the trunnion, wounded five men and went through the mid gun deck, where it was taken up in a bucket and thrown overboard. It was perfectly red hot and burned the deck as it rolled about.

Nov. 5. Ordered to move ship out of range.

„ 8. Received from the Arsenal a large pontoon.

„ 11. Enemy still diverting themselves by firing at us.

„ 12. Finding enemy's shot still going over us, moved Eastward.

„ 14. Enemy with a very long gun they have got fired several shot over our masthead and which went so far beyond us that I am certain it throws at least 3 miles.

„ 30. Capture of Battery, but unfortunately a party of the Royals whose zeal got the better of the rules of good order, pursued the flying troops of the enemy and being followed by other troops of the allied army, threw the whole into confusion, which the enemy taking advantage of in their turn, with a very large reinforcement, attacked our troops, killed and wounded the greatest part of those who had separated themselves from the main body, and repossessed themselves of the height and Battery before any of the guns were spiked.

Dec. 17. Capture of Fort Mulgrave. The enemy put nearly the whole of the garrison to the sword, very few escaping. The number of the British amounted to about 250, the rest Spaniards. The Neapolitan camp, consisting together with the reinforcement from the town of about 1500, kept the enemy at a stand till about 7, when it was determined to withdraw all the troops from that Post. All the launches and other craft being ready to embark them received orders with the 'Nemesis' and 'Ariadne' to cover them, for which purpose got out springs and brought our guns to bear. By 10.30 the whole of the troops were embarked without any loss...at noon got everything in readiness to move the ship, being within musket shot of two batterys now in the enemy's possession.

„ 18. The launch employed taking the sick and wounded from the Hospital...the poor inhabitants are flocking on board the ships, in the greatest numbers, begging to be received.

„ 19. 1 p.m. Weighed and towed out of the Road; some of the boats bringing the troops from Sepet. At 4 anchored. At 9 sent all the boats of the fleet to Fort Lewis to embark the troops from Fort La Malgue, being the last of them on shore. At that time the ships in the Arsenal were on fire as well as the Arsenal itself. At 1.30 one of the frigates with powder blow up with a prodigious explosion. At 2 p.m. the whole of the troops were embarked without loss, boats of all descriptions bringing on board emigrants. At 6 weighed.

Dec. 21. Transporting troops from one ship to another and disposing of emigrants, sending husbands to look after wives in other ships, and wives for their husbands and children, for the very short warning these poor people had, occasioned the greatest confusion, many women even hanging by boats to secure a passage to the ships leaving their property behind.

'ST GEORGE' (Log of Master, Thos. Ball).

June 20. At 10 arrived V. Adm. Hood in the 'Victory' and V. Adm. Hotham in the 'Britannia' and part of their fleet (at Gibraltar).

,, 24. At 10 arrived 'Agamemnon,' 'Courageux,' 'Leviathan,' 'Robust,' 'Fortitude,' 'Colossus.'

,, 27. Sailed.

July 8. Ivica.

,, 10. West end Minorca.

,, 12. East end Majorca.

,, 15. Toulon N. 50, E. 49 miles.

,, 30. N.W. end Corsica.

Aug. 7. Cape Sepet N.E. 4 leagues.

,, 28. Wore ship and brought to at 7; boats all employed landing the troops.

,, 30. Came to anchor in Toulon Harbour, half a cable from flagstaff of fort on W. side of Harbour. Spanish fleet anchored to Eastward of us.

Sept. 20. At 11 the floating Battery fired several shot. A.m. strong gales. The enemy opened two new Batterys on us. Beat to quarters. We with the 'Aurora' fired on the enemy. At 8 one of our lower deck guns burst, which killed and wounded 20 men. At 11 both the floating Batteries were obliged to slip their cables. At noon having silenced one of the enemy's Batterys, ceased firing.

,, 21. At 2 the enemy employed repairing their forts. We with the 'Aurora' fired upon them and continued to do so until 5. The 'Aurora' and one fort fired at each other till 6. Got on board several French boats laden with powder and shot at 7. Strong gales. We were obliged to slip our springs. At 2 one of the floating Batterys sunk.

,, 23. Strong gales. Two Spanish ships of the line and the two floating Batteries fired upon the enemy's works at 8. We fired upon do. and continued to do so till noon.

,, 24. At one recommenced firing on the enemy. Several shells were thrown into their works. At 4 we fired on the town of La Seyne; several shells were thrown into do. At 8 unmoored; at noon waying out of Harbour.

[Log ends 29th Sept.]

COMMANDER'S log.

Oct.　1. Sailed at 8 in company with 'Bedford,' 'Captain,' 'Mermaid,' 'Tartar,' 'Conflagration,' 'Vulcan,' 'Alert' brig, and 'Scipion.'

,,　5. At 6 working into Genoa; at noon 'Bedford' took possession of French frigate and two gunboats. The Fort saluted us.

Nov. 3. Sailed.

,,　10. Anchored Toulon.

,,　21. Sailed.

,,　30. Arrived Gibraltar; 'Colossus' in company.

Jan.　1. 1794. Sailed.

'WINDSOR CASTLE' (Log of Captain Sir Thos. Byard).

Hamoaze to 30 March; Spithead 2 April; St Helens 16 April; Lizard 27 April; Finisterre 7 May; Gibraltar 15 May. With Hood after; Genoa 16 Aug.

Aug. 29. A detachment of troops, marines and seamen took possession of Fort Louis.

Oct.　1. Sent to Fort La Malgue Lieut. midshipman and 20 men. Returned 2nd.

,,　17. Stood out to sea in company with a Neapolitan 74 and three frigates, a French frigate and 13 transports.

,,　23. Vado Bay.

,,　31. Port Espacia [Spezzia].

Nov. 21. Leghorn Road. Found riding here H.M. frigates 'Meleager' and 'Amphitrite' with the 'Tancredi,' 'Arethusa' and 'Tome,' Neapolitan ships of war; 'Scipion' and 'Proselyte,' French ships of war.

,,　27. Observed 'Scipion' to be on fire; sent all boats, 2.30.

,,　28. Wreck still burning.

Dec.　6. Toulon.

,,　16. Heavy firing between Fort Mulgrave and Malbosquet and the enemy.
3 a.m. 'Victory' made signal for all boats. 6.2 firing ceased. Sent Lieut. 2 petty officers and 29 men to Fort Mulgrave.

,,　17. Boats employed embarking troops from Fort Balaghue.

,,　18. At 5 p.m. Fort Pomet blown up by our people by order. Recd. our men and officers from Fort Pomet. Brought off the sick and wounded from the Hospital.

,,　19. At 1 p.m. weighed and towed ship out of the Road. Embarking troops from Cape Sepet. 8 p.m. sent all boats on shore.

APPENDIX D

INSTRUCTIONS TO THE ROYAL COMMISSIONERS AT TOULON (LORD HOOD, GENERAL O'HARA, AND SIR GILBERT ELLIOT)[1]

[Précis.]   Whitehall, October 18.

The Comms. will administer Toulon and its dependencies, and try to induce other parts of France to rely on H.M.'s protection. They will publish at Toulon a Declaration, the articles of which are explained. The first article deals with the restoration of Toulon to Louis XVII at the peace, subject however to "the conditions which H.M. will be justly entitled to expect for himself and his Allies." The second assures the Toulonese of adequate succour. The third adds details, private assurance being added as to the despatch of British troops (raising their total to 3000 infantry and a regiment of cavalry) also of 5000 Hessians. Allied reinforcements are being pressed for so as to enable offensive moves to be made. The Comms. will provide for the protection of life and property at Toulon and decide on topics such as the meetings of the Sections and the expulsion of suspects. The fourth article asserts H.M.'s primary object to be that of ending the war "on just, secure and honourable grounds," but whatever may be the form of government in France, he and his Allies are entitled to "reasonable indemnification for the past and security for the future." He will make peace with and protect those parts of France which declare for hereditary monarchy, restoring them at the peace, unless they "shall for the purpose of indemnification or security be ceded to" any of the Allies. No dismemberment is intended, but only the cession of certain frontier districts, particularly to Austria, Spain or Sardinia, or to Switzerland in case she joins the Allies. This must be made known as widely as possible at Toulon and in the interior of France.

H.M. is convinced that regular government in France can be assured only by the restoration of monarchy in the person of Louis XVII, but considers its benefits to depend on the adoption of just limitations, without, however, in any way upholding those prescribed in 1789, many of which will be seen to be impracticable. All places which accept H.M.'s protection "must be considered as for the time in H.M.'s possession and subject to his supreme authority"; and the authority of any of the French princes, even in the character of Regent, cannot be admitted, unless by special arrangement. The

---

[1] For the text almost in full, see Cottin, pp. 419–25.

Commissioners will, however, interfere as little as possible with the ordinary course of local affairs; but they will restore confiscated property and raise troops as seems desirable.

INSTRUCTIONS TO HOOD AND O'HARA.

Whitehall, October 18.

By their commission they are to act jointly with Sir G. Elliot who will deal specifically with matters of a civil and political nature. It is proper that Hood should be named as the head of the commission, but he and O'Hara will be chiefly occupied with their military duties, and it would be incompatible with these to conduct the various extensive and political details connected with the present situation of affairs in the South of France, which are to be left to Sir G. Elliot. It will nevertheless be desirable for them to confer with him as occasion may require on the most important questions that may arise. H.M. relies on their exercising this joint commission with that harmony and mutual confidence which is essential to its success.

APPENDIX E

LORD HOOD'S CORRESPONDENCE

In May—December, 1793

HOOD TO H. DUNDAS.

Portsmouth, May 21.

Acknowledges receipt of a confidential letter of 19th inst. with a copy of the Anglo-Sardinian treaty and of a secret article of same.

HOOD TO P. STEPHENS (Secretary to the Admiralty).

'Victory,' at sea, June 7.

Has just fallen in with the Mediterranean convoy of 76 sail, will see it safe within the Lizard, and then proceed to Gibraltar.

HOOD TO ST HELENS.

'Victory,' off Cape St Mary's [near Cadiz], June 14.

Informs Lord St Helens, British ambassador at Madrid, that convoy duties have detained him, but he will soon enter the Mediterranean and make for Toulon. Desires close co-operation with the Allies, subject to his main duty, "which is that of seeking and giving battle to the fleet of France and of securing to H.M.'s subjects and those of his Allies the free and uninterrupted navigation of the Mediterranean." Will arrange with the K. of Sardinia a plan for the recovery of Nice. (For the text in full see *The Naval Miscellany* (N.R.S.), I, 235–7.)

LORD ST HELENS TO GRENVILLE.

Madrid, July 3.

[In cypher.] I observe from Lord Hood's letter[1] that he objects strongly to the idea of his acting in any way in absolute conjunction with a Spanish squadron, and that he is of opinion that, in case the two Powers should agree on undertaking any joint enterprise, it would be better that it should be conducted by one of the two squadrons, and that the other should be employed in watching and keeping in check the naval force of the enemy. This plan would in fact obviate a number of difficulties, and it seems to be sufficiently conformable to the notions entertained here. However, in case the

---

[1] Not enclosed.

Cadiz squadron should be ordered to the Mediterranean, I rather think, as it will be much inferior in strength, if not in numbers, to that of Admiral Borja, this Court will be desirous that it should cruize either in company with the British squadron, or so near it as to be at all times sure of its protection. I hope to be able to obtain from the Spanish Minister some explanation of his views on that head, which I shall not fail to communicate to Y. Lp. as well as to Lord Hood, with whom I mean to correspond thro' the channel of H.M.'s consul at Genoa.

HOOD TO P. STEPHENS.

'Victory,' off C. Cicie, July 15.

Voyage up the Medn. has been most tedious, 19 days from Gibraltar: met Span. squadron off Iviça at night; gave and received in answer the secret signals agreed on, and sent by Ld. St Helens; was courteously welcomed. Order of Battle of the Spanish Fleet in Medn. under Don Borja.—26 sail of line and 10 frigates.

HON. JOHN TREVOR TO HOOD.

Turin, Tuesday night, July 21.

[Acknowledges receipt of Hood's letters of June 26 and July 16[1] brought by Capt. Inglefield in 'l'Aigle' to Genoa yesterday and forwarded by express. Hood and Trevor can easily correspond through Oneglia.] ...I am sorry to say that things are much altered for the worse in this part of the world since I had the honour to write to Y. Lp. in February last when I flattered myself that the moment of the appearance of the British fleet in the Mediterranean was much nearer at hand; the enemy is grown considerably stronger both by sea and land; besides 17 or 18,000 men in the County of Nice, he has had time to erect fortifications upon every access towards the town[2], and along the coast, whilst on the other hand the force on this side is very considerably diminished by sickness and desertion, and the very material reinforcements from the Milanese have hitherto been withheld by the shortsighted policy of the Court of Vienna or by the personal jealousies and intrigues against General Devins. We have not at this moment above 7000 Austrian Allies and not more than 20,000 Piedmontese troops that can be called in any degree *disposable*. This situation of affairs obliges me to say in general that in the present moment no measure of co-operation with Y. Lp. can be undertaken till we are considerably stronger on this side by the arrival of more Austrians. [Encouragement caused by the arrival of Hood's fleet.]

---

[1] These I have not found.   [2] The town of Nice.

SAME TO SAME.

Turin, July 22.

...I find that Masseria, Paoli's great confidential friend, was arrived at Leghorn. The Tuscan Govt., at which I am indignant, obliged him to withdraw from thence. I believe he went to Genoa, and I daresay will take the first opportunity of joining Y. Lp. and informing you of the situation of affairs, and of the wish of that island [Corsica] to recover its independence under the protection of Great Britain. The French have about a dozen of frigates out on hearing of the retreat of the Spaniards. Three sailed, just before Y. Lp. arrived off Toulon, for Leghorn; the 'Modeste' of 40 guns and 'Badine' of 30 are at Genoa. They have five in the Levant, four at Smyrna, and one at Salonica, at Tunis a 74, four frigates and three corvettes, and two stout ships at Corsica.

HOOD TO P. STEPHENS.

'Victory,' off Toulon, July 27.

On the 19th inst. a heavy gale came on and lasted three days: fleet lost three topmasts; 'Robust' sprang her mainmast; 'Berwick,' to leeward, parted company: fleet was scattered and could with difficulty rejoin: 'Meleager' had to make for Mahon.

TREVOR TO HOOD.

Genoa, Monday morning, July 29.

Describes the conduct of the 'Modeste' and 'Badine,' which prevented H.M.S. 'Aigle' from leaving Genoa harbour.

J. N. INGLEFIELD TO HOOD.

'L'Aigle,' Genoa, July 29.

[Having finished his conference with the Chevr. de Revel yesterday Evg. (at which Mr Trevor was present), he unmoored and was about to stand out with the land breeze.] ...Two French frigates, the 'Modeste' of 40 guns, and 'Badine' of 30, are in this port, destined to convoy some vessels laden with corn. The shape of the Mole makes it unavoidable to moor otherwise than close alongside of each other; in this situation they had, until we attempted to move, behaved with decency; but about nine, last night, upon our heaving out of the Mole, they instantly unmoored, hoisted their yards up and hove so close to us that, had the ships swung different ways, we must have been on board each other, and in their condition of clamour and madness I think we must have come to blows. This morning have charged Mr Brame to deliver a complaint in writing to the Government....The Sardinian frigate ['St Victor'] is in a disarmed state without powder, and her men at another port, with a wooden bottom; and the Genoese exceedingly jealous of her motions; it is therefore agreed that, until we have a superior force, that she cannot be moved. [He urges the despatch of such a force in order to cut off the food supplies to Nice, where the French are in a wretched condition.]

LORD CHATHAM TO HOOD.

Admiralty, August 1.

I did not receive your letter by the 'Fox' Cutter till the 22nd ult., nor the duplicate till the 25th, which seem to have come slowly, so that I hope before very long to hear a further account of your progress up the Mediterranean. I rejoiced to hear of your safe arrival at Gibraltar, and that upon the whole, (the Levanter excepted) you had so good a passage, tho' I fear you must have been very unpleasantly detained in the Channel looking out for the convoy with the 'Assistance.' I am very glad that the Ships you sent into Cadiz were so well received, and think Langara's letter, a copy of which you sent me, seemed to be very cordial and friendly, and I hope a good understanding will continue between us, at the same time the proposal for the fleet to act separately seems the most desirable arrangement. I have nothing at all material to communicate to you as yet respecting any further arrangements, as nothing new has arisen hitherto to vary the general objects on which we have so often conversed. I regret much that you found the naval hospital at Gibraltar in so bad a state and wonder how it escaped us to give particular directions on the subject, previous to your sailing. I am very anxious to hear what the real situation is of the French force at Toulon, of which we have very little and very imperfect intelligence. They have a considerable number of Ships in the Bay [outside Brest], and there seems every reason to hope that Lord Howe may shortly be able to attack them. We are all here very impatient for further accounts from the West Indies: there is hardly a chance that the Royalists at Martinique may be strong enough to enable us to take possession of the island with the small land force we have there, but it seems scarcely probable, and I should rather think no attempts can be effectually made against the French islands till after the hurricane months. The French fleet seen by Captain Sinclair, has never been heard of more, and the doubt in which this matter yet remains is very singular. We shall begin to look out for the 'Aquilon' soon, and which I trust will arrive without any accident. You will I am sure have heard with great pleasure of the brilliant action of the 'La Nymph'[1]. That of the 'Iris,' by your account seems to have been a severe one, and it is much to be regretted, that the unfortunate loss

[1] On June 17 'Nymphe' (40—Capt. Pellew) took 'Cléopatre (36) in 50 minutes (James, I, 106–109).

of his mast, prevented Captain Lumsdaine's ultimate Success[1]. I am happy to hear Rennet is recovering and that you have been so good to take him into the 'Victory.' We have received the welcome account of the Surrender of Mentz to the King of Prussia, and of Valenciennes to the Combined Armies, and fortunately with less loss than it was apprehended, it must have cost. Their next operation probably will be the siege of Dunkirk. It remains to be seen what effects these events may produce on the minds of people in France, hitherto [they?] seem to resist the powerful Confederacy against them with great obstinacy. Adieu, My Dear Lord.

HOOD TO JOSEPH BRAME (Consul at Genoa).

'Victory,' Coast of Savoy [Oneglia], August 4.

From the Report that has been made to me of the very indecent extraordinary and unprecedented behaviour of two captains of French frigates in the mole of Genoa, when one of H.B.M.'s ships was attempting to sail in the evening of the 28th of last month, which you have been fully informed of by her commander (Captain Inglefield) and by whose prudence in laying fast much serious mischief was prevented, for had he persisted in weighing the ship's anchor she must have inevitably been entangled with the French frigate; I am under the necessity of requiring you in the most formal and forcible manner to represent the conduct of the captains of said frigates to the Genoese Governt., which I make no doubt will notice in a proper manner so flagrant a breach of the rules and regulations invariably observed in all neutral ports by ships of different nations at war. I shall wait upon this coast the result of the representations I feel it very much my duty to desire you will immediately make.

HOOD TO DE REVEL AT GENOA.

'Victory,' off Genoa, August 10.

I received on the 8th inst. by Captain Inglefield the very obliging letter you did me the honor to write me on the 28th of last month, and I shall feel myself extremely happy to avail myself of any and every opportunity that may offer, of giving the full force of the Fleet under my command in support of any plan of operation His Sardinian Majesty may adopt for the recovery of Nice. But I am at present unable to see, how far I can effectually be of use to H.M.'s views, farther than for a very short time to cover any body of troops, that may be judged necessary to be landed upon the sea coast: None of the ships of my fleet have troops on board, beyond a party serving in lieu of marines, as part of their complements, it will not therefore be in my power, to put any of them on shore; nor can I with propriety divide my ships of the line, beyond three or four days at a time whilst

---

[1] 'Iris' *v.* 'Citoyenne Française' on May 13 (James, I, 100–102).

the enemy is so evidently strong at Toulon. But I judged it of use to shew myself off Nice and Genoa with a part of my fleet, having left the remainder off the Islands of Hières, and, before the French can know of my coming here, so as to put to sea, I can be back again off their Port.

There is nothing Sir I have more at heart than to render substantial service to the King of Sardinia. But I have been instructed to believe, that a plan of operations was to be concerted by the Ambassadors of the allied powers, and when finally arranged and settled the Fleet of Spain, and Naples, and that of England, would have its distinct line of acting; the one to watch the port of Toulon, and the other to attend and support whatever attacks should be judged expedient to make for driving the French out of Savoy, which I humbly conceive to be the first object to be attended to; neither fleet is equal to both services at the same time. You must be aware, Sir, that every place where a ship can put her Head has Guns mounted, and a few accidental shot may so cripple the masts, as to make her totally unserviceable. The object therefore should be well considered before a Fleet is hazarded, with a superior one at hand ready to put to Sea. I shall now send three Ships of the Line and as many frigates to Genoa, to fill what water they can in three days, and the moment they rejoin me, I shall return before Toulon, if not before. I have given directions to Capn. Linzee of the 'Alcide,' to liberate the King of Sardinia's Frigate, to afford Coll. Ross what assistance he may require and to see him safe to Oneglia[1].

HOOD TO P. STEPHENS.

'Victory,' off Ventimiglia, August 11.

Thinking the Toulon fleet will not come out for the present, he will show the flag off Genoa; has sent 'Ardent,' 'Romney' and 'Leda' to Leghorn for provisions, etc., and trusts that V. Adm. Cosby's visit to Genoa will bring her to observe neutrality. Hood will then return off Toulon; he has taken steps to intercept a French 74 and frigates at Tunis.

MULGRAVE TO HOOD.

Turin, August 13.

I arrived at this Place on the 10th of this Month, having been delay'd twelve Days on my Journey by a variety of accidents. Mr Secretary Dundas informed me on my quitting London that he had transmitted to Y. Lp. a Copy of my Instructions; I am extremely anxious to fulfil that part of them which directs an immediate communication with Y. Lp. so soon as I shall have obtained any informa-

[1] The 'St Victor' was detained in Genoa harbour by the French frigate 'Modeste' and her consorts.

tion worthy of your notice, or received any plan of operations which may merit Y. Lp.'s consideration, for the advancement of the common cause. Toulon, Marseilles, and Corsica are the main objects pointed at in my Instructions, for information respecting the latter I was particularly referred to Capt. Masseria, but I have not yet been able to learn where he is to be found.

My Instructions were calculated in a great degree on the supposition of the Enemy being already driven from the County of Nice, but from present State of the Troops [?] in this Country I fear it will require considerable exertions of co-operation, and some reinforcement of the army on the Frontiers of Piedmont, to effect even the evacuation of Nice before the close of the present campaign; I purpose to go immediately to the different posts of the Sardinian Army; and to collect with every possible expedition all the information I can procure in this quarter; with which I shall, without delay, repair on board of the 'Victory' to consult with Y. Lp. on the different objects of my Mission.

HOOD TO P. STEPHENS.

'Victory,' off Oneglia, August 14 (rec. September 8).

I have been strongly pressed to station a frigate at Leghorn and Genoa, to bring despatches from those places, which I am unable to do, from the more important services I have for them. I have sent one of the little hired cutters in lieu, and appointed a trusty lieutenant to each....I have just received certain intelligence that the French have six frigates cruising off the Island of Cerigo at the entrance of the Archipelago for the purpose of intercepting our convoys to and from Smyrna, Salonica &c. I have therefore added 'L'Aimable' to the ships under Captain Inglefield as convoy to that Trade; and I have written to Sir William Hamilton to desire he will propose to the King of Naples that directions may be given to two of H.M.'s frigates being put under Captain Inglefield's orders. The 'St Albans,' with the Trade bound to England from Leghorn and Genoa, are now in sight. I shall therefore keep in the rear of the convoy until it gets to the westward of Toulon, as the French have three stout frigates at Villafranca, and the 74 and several frigates are daily expected from Tunis.

DE REVEL TO HOOD.

[Translation.]

Genoa, August 18.

I have communicated to my Court the answer which Y. Lp. honored me with, the 10th of this month. The King received with much satisfaction the new assurances of your disposition to second the operations which may be thought advantageous to his interests and to those of the common cause; and I am commanded to testify to you, H.M.'s high sense of the protection which the Ships under your command, gave to the frigate[1] at Genoa. H.M., My Lord, is sensible of the just considerations which require the presence of your fleet before Toulon, and which do not permit you to detach ships of the line for any considerable time. It is upon these principles that the King has ordered that the attacks against the French army may be combined. Lord Mulgrave is occupied with this plan, and as I have been informed he intends to visit Y. Lp. in order to communicate the particulars of what should be done. In pursuance of the orders given me I have the honor to lay before Y. Lp. the general points upon which H.M. desires, and hopes to have the cooperation of a part of your force.

The proposition which Y. Lp. made to Mr Trevor to keep frigates cruizing between Oneglia and Nice to intercept all the vessels bound to the ports in the possession of the French and to protect the corsairs belonging to Oneglia, would contribute to prevent the Coasting Trade. This proposition was very agreeable to H.M., since it is well known that famine is the army the least expensive for the Allies, and at the same time the most powerful to reduce the French. These frigates without being diverted from their object would protect the landing proposed to the East of Villa Franca near to Eza (?), of which I made mention formerly.

H.M. would desire likewise that at the time of the attacks, some English ships might make a simple feint for landing troops at Cagne [Cannes?], in order to give inquietude to the enemy, and to make them retain the troops stationed at that place: it might be accomplished without the ships being put into a dangerous situation; you will perceive My Lord, that, if the number and quality of the vessels necessary is not determined, the effect to be expected from this menace will however be in proportion to the number of ships employed.

The delays which the answers have incurred, the resolution of Lord Mulgrave to make himself acquainted with the places where the operations will begin, and afterwards to wait upon Y. Lp., may necessarily put off the execution of it till towards the end of this month or beginning of September. The news from Nice give us reason to believe that the French will be driven from it, if they do not evacuate it before being attacked, and many circumstances lead us to believe that it is their design. They attacked our posts the 4th of this month, but so feebly, that had not a fog occurred, which obscured everything, our troops would have certainly had great advantages over the disorder in which they were at first put. Since that time, the French Battalions have passed the Var, also 40 pieces of Cannon. Our troops have dislodged the French from some villages which were strongly occupied, and they voluntarily abandoned some posts that were essential to their defence. The Commissioners of the Convention have arrested, and chained General Brunet. I suppose,

---

[1] The Sardinian frigate, 'St Victor.'

without being very certain, that it was because the Commissioners wished to employ this Army, at least part, against the Marsellois, and that the General opposed this measure. Sickness, famine, and particularly desertion still prevail in the French Army. This situation of affairs makes us entertain great hopes that the operations projected will produce the evacuation of the whole of Nice.

 Je soussigné, Jean Joseph André Abeille, chargé de pleins pouvoirs du Comité de Sureté generale de Marseilles, établi par les corps administratifs et les sections de la dite ville, prie le Cap. John Woodley d'offrir a son Ex. Admiral Hood les vœux des habitants du Dept. des Bouches du Rhone pour le retablissement de la monarchie en France par le regne de Louis XVII, fils du feu Louis XVI.

Je m'engage en ma dite qualité de faire proclamer mon dit seigneur et roi dans toute l'étendue du dit Dept. dès que son Ex. l'Adm. Hood aura bien voulu prêter les Forces qui sont sous ses ordres pour appuyer et defendre les intentions de mes commettans qui m'ont expressement chargé de les faire connoitre dans toute leur purete.

Sd. J. Abeille.

Faite abord de la Frégate de S.M.B. 'Nemesis,' le 22 Aout, 1793[1].

DRAFT FROM LORDS COMMISSIONERS TO HOOD.

Whitehall, August 23.

The messenger brings instructions concerning the treaty concluded with the King of Naples. Enclosed is copy of a letter from Captain Masseria who was employed during the late war in the corps of Corsicans at Gibraltar, was associated with Paoli both before and after that time and lived with him in London, leaving there about four years ago, to return to Corsica. Uncertain what he has done since he left England, but probably he can be usefully employed on any measures that may be taken with respect to Corsica. He is a man of ability, and in previous intercourse there was no reason to complain of his conduct. He was employed to watch over some other foreigners. It is now of great importance that Hood should endeavour to place himself on an advantageous footing with the Court of Naples, and he should therefore open a confidential communication with that Court, through Sir Wm Hamilton. But it is not meant that this communication should be perfectly unreserved, but sufficient only to carry an appearance of his confidence in their good disposition, and not to extend to anything necessary for him to keep to himself, or proper for the information of those only with whom he is immediately to act.

---

[1] Enclosure in Hood's letter of October 27 to H. Dundas.

HOOD TO P. STEPHENS.

'Victory,' off the Islands of Hières, August 25

(rec. September 13).

Be pleased to acquaint the Lords Comms. of the Admy. that on the 23rd Commissioners from Marseilles came with full powers from the Sections of the Mouths of the Rhone to treat for peace. They expected to be met by Commissioners from Toulon deputed by the Sections of the Var; upon which (the Commissioners, having clearly and explicitly declared their views to be in favour of Monarchy) I sent on shore to Toulon and Marseilles the Proclamation and Preliminary Declaration I have now the honour to inclose copies of[1]. The former was intended to make an impression on the minds of the populace, who are the Government of France. The Toulon Comms. are now on board and have offered to put the harbour and forts in my possession; but at present I have not troops sufficient to defend the works, and there is a strong division in the [French] fleet. I am however about to anchor in the Bay of Hières, as the batteries in the islands are secured. This will enable me to be at hand to assist the Royalists. Had I 5 or 6000 good troops with me the war would soon be at an end.

The day previous to the arrival of the Commissioners from Marseilles I had written to Don Borja, who, I was told, was off Cape Creuse acquainting him that want of water would oblige me to go into port the end of this month, and hoped to have the honour of seeing him in a few days to guard Toulon. But it seems Don Langara commands the fleet of Spain in these seas, who has told me in a letter I have within this hour received from him, that his Instructions will not allow him to leave the service he is upon. I have however sent the frigate back to him, requesting him in the most pressing manner that in the present situation of things (which I have fully stated to him) he will be pleasend to send the squadron of his fleet under the command of Adm. Gravina to me with as many troops as he can spare. I have also written to Sir William Hamilton, asking the Neapolitan ships and troops, and likewise to Mr Trevor at Turin (under whose cover I send this to be forwarded) for the information of the King of Sardinia, as I have been informed a great party [sic] of the army that was in Savoy is now marching against Toulon.

P.S. An officer is just come off with an account that the white flag was this day hoisted on all the forts and on part of the Fleet, and that those ships that did not do so were fired at from the forts. I long to know the issue, which I shall do in the morning as three of the Comms. are gone on shore for the purpose.

[1] They are in the *Ann. Reg.* for 1793.

SAME TO SAME.

'Victory,' August 26 (rec. September 13).

It being perfectly calm since sealing my letter of yesterday's date, I take up my pen to acquaint you that the forts did not fire upon the ships in the harbour as was reported. A captain of one of the ships of the line is now on board and tells me that 11 of the 17 great ships in the roads are commanded by violent democrats. Trogoff is superseded in the command of the fleet, retired to the fort, and a St Julien of a turbulent mind appointed in his room. The French army in Italy is in full march against Toulon[1], but I trust that of the King of Sardinia will be soon at its heels.

ADM. LANGARA TO HOOD.

'Mexicano,' off the coast of Roussillon, August 26.

I have received Y. Ex.'s much esteemed letter with the intelligence therein mentioned and enclosing a copy of your Proclamation. In consequence I cannot resist taking the greatest interest in the common cause and considering the effects that might result from my not taking advantage of so favourable an opportunity, I have determined to proceed immediately in view of your squadron and at the same time I despatched an express to the Commander in Chief of the Army in Roussillon, desiring that he would embark in four ships, which I left for that purpose, 2 or 3000 of the best troops, to be employed as Y. Ex. wishes in the operations you have pointed out.

PROCLAMATION BY LORD HOOD.

'Victory,' off Toulon, August 28.

Whereas the Sections of Toulon have by their Commissioners to me made a solemn declaration in favour of Monarchy, have proclaimed Louis XVII, son of the late Louis XVI their lawfull king and have sworn to acknowledge him and no longer suffer the Despotism of the Tyrants which at this time govern France, but will do their utmost to establish monarchy as accepted by their late sovereign in 1789 and restore Peace to their distracted and calamitous country: I do hereby repeat what I have already declared to the people of the South of France that I take possession of Toulon and hold it in

---

[1] Incorrect. The Commissioners of the Convention ordered General Brunet, commanding the Republican army in the County of Nice, to detach a division for the recapture of Toulon. Not having enough men to spare, he refused; and for this reason was later on guillotined. A division under La Barre was however soon despatched and it occupied the village of La Valette, east of Toulon.

trust only for Louis XVII until Peace shall be reestablished in France, which I hope and trust will be soon.

[For Hood's and Langara's joint Proclamation of September 4 to the French troops in the South of France, see *Naval Chron.* 1799, pp. 112–4.]

HOOD TO P. STEPHENS.

'Victory,' in the Road of Toulon, August 29 (rec. September 15).

In my letter of the 25th (of which I herewith send a duplicate and also of its enclosures) I had the honor to acquaint you, for the information of the Lords Commrs. of the Admiralty, of the situation of things at Toulon and Marseilles. Since that, several messages have passed between me and the Sections of Toulon, and having assurances that they had proclaimed Louis XVII king and had sworn to acknowledge him and no longer suffer the despotism of the Tyrants which at this time govern France, and that they would be zealous in their endeavours to restore peace to their distracted and calamitous country, I came to the resolution of landing 1500 men, and take possession of the forts which command the ships in the Road. St Julien, a turbulent hot headed democrat (to whom the seamen had given the command of the fleet in the room of Trogoff) had the command of the forts on the left of the Harbour, and declared resistance.

In all enterprises of war danger more or less is to be expected and must be submitted to; but impressed with the great importance of taking possession of Toulon, the great fort of Malgue and others on the main, in shortening the war, I fully relied that in case my endeavour should not succeed, I should be justified in running some risque, being conscious I acted to the best of my judgment as a faithful servant to my king and country. Therefore at midnight on the 27th I made the necessary arrangements for putting the troops on shore as near as possible to the great fort, without their being molested by those batteries in the hand of St Julien, under the immediate protection of the 'Meleager' and 'Tartar,' supported by the 'Egmont,' 'Robust,' 'Courageux' and 'Colossus,' which were all in the fort by noon on the 28th; and I authorised Capt. Elphinstone to land and enter at the head of the troops the fort of Malgue and to take upon him the charge and command as governor; and directed Capt. Dickson, on his anchoring, to send a flag with peremptory notice to St Julien that such ships as did not immediately proceed into the inner Harbour and put their powder on shore, should be treated as enemies. All but seven, whose crews ran off with St Julien, removed in the course of the day.

It is impossible for me to express my obligation to Don Langara, adequate to my feelings of it, for the singular honor of his implicit confidence in and good opinion of me in the promptitude his Ex. manifested to comply with the wishes contained in my second letter;

as his Ex. was not content with sending Adm. Gravina, but came with his whole squadron except four, which he left to bring a body of troops from the army at Rosellon [Roussillon]; and made his appearance from the deck of the 'Victory' as the troops from H.M.'s squadron under my command were in the act of landing. Adm. Gravina come on board, and upon my explaining to him the necessity of as many Spanish troops being put on shore immediately as could be spared, he told me he was authorised by his Admiral to pay attention to any request I should make and undertook to prepare a thousand at least, to be landed this morning under the protection of the four ships I had ordered to anchor and were all in the fort before 12 o'clock.

I herewith transmit a copy of Don Langara's letter in answer to mine of the 25th. The corps of Cartau has been at Marseilles and committed all manner of enormities, and is now on its march to Toulon, expecting to join the army near at hand from Italy. The former consists of 10,000 men, the number of the latter is not ascertained, but, be it more or less, I trust the whole will make no impression even upon the town of Toulon; upon the fort of Malgue I am pretty confident they cannot do it. Information has just been sent me that Cartau has planned to send away from Marseilles all the money as well as merchandise in the town, the former is said to consist of four million of livres, but I have planned to prevent him by having sent off Marseilles two ships of the Line, with orders not to suffer any vessel to sail; and I am now sending two frigates, which I could not spare before. After having taken possession of Toulon and the forts I judged it expedient to issue another proclamation which Capt. Elphinstone tells me has had a very happy effect, a copy of which I also enclose. The knowledge of this event to the king and H.M.'s ministers appears to me of that magnitude that I think it expedient to adopt two modes of conveyance, one by way of Barcelona, and the other Genoa. Lord Hugh Conway has the charge of one despatch and the Hon. Capt. Waldegrave the other, who will be able to inform H.M.'s ministers at those places they may pass, of the Allied Powers.

P.S. I have just received the Address from a very numerous and respectable body of gentlemen I have now the honor to transmit[1].

HOOD TO P. STEPHENS.
'Victory,' Outer Road of Toulon, September 1.

In the critical situation I at present am [in], it must be very satisfactory to the Lords Comms. of the Admy. to have frequent accounts from me. Yesterday afternoon a part of Carteaux' Army, consisting of 750 men, approached near Toulon: Captain Elphinstone whom I had appointed Governor of the great fort of Malgue and its dependencies, marched out at the head of 600 troops and put it to the

[1] See *Naval Chron.* 1799, and *Ann. Reg.* 1793.

rout, took four pieces of cannon, their ammunition, &c. I have herewith the honour to send you Governor Elphinstone's letter[1], and most exceedingly lament the loss of a very excellent officer, Major Douglas, who I had appointed Town Major, and whose zeal for going out with the troops could not be restrained. The ball entered his breast and was extracted at the shoulder blade. He died last night. Upon the troops leaving the fort, the appointed signal was made for a number of seamen that were kept ready, and 400 were on shore immediately to put the Fort out of danger. This check will make Carteaux keep his distance, and am very confident we can hold what we have got against a thousand Carteaux. Vigilance, however, is necessary in every quarter; and as the town of Toulon and the great fort of Malgue and those dependent on it are too much for any one man to give proper attention to, R. Adm. Goodall is so obliging as to take upon him the charge and command of Governor and R. Adm. Gravina that of Commander of the Troops[2].

It is with very singular satisfaction that I have the honour to inform you that there is a most perfect and cordial good understanding subsisting between Adm. Langara and me. Yesterday in great form we exchanged visits; each left his ship at the same moment and rowed alongside that of the other, attended by their junior Flags and were saluted.

On our return we met, and civilities passed, when I went into Don Langara's boat and received him on board the 'Victory': from thence we went on shore together, first to Malgue, and next to the town, where we were received with all appearance of very joyful hearts. The keys were presented to me, when I announced to all the Sections that Adm. Langara and I (standing close to each other) were only *One*: that we were actuated by the same principles, and came to give protection to the good and loyal people of the south of France: that it would be their own faults if they were not saved from impending misery and distress, as they had only to submit to the regulations we had made and implicitly obey orders: then R. Adm. Goodall was presented as Governor and R. Adm. Gravina as Commandant of the Troops. The enclosed is a copy of an intercepted letter this moment sent me by the Committee of Safety at Toulon[3].

P.S. The signal is this moment, for the Convoy's being in sight, with a considerable body of Spanish troops from the Army in Roussillon.

Sir W. Hamilton to Hood.

Naples, September 1.

I have been honor'd with Y. Lp.'s letters of the 11th and 12th ultimo, by the return of the Neapolitan Pilot, and immediately communicated their contents to General Acton, His Sicilian Majesty's

---

[1] In *Naval Chron.* of 1799.   [2] Cottin prints this despatch only from here.
[3] In *Naval Chron.* of 1799, p. 110.

Minister for Foreign Affairs, and who is likewise at the head of the War, and Marine Departments. Y. Lp. will see by the inclosed Copy of H. Ex.'s Answer, that there is the utmost desire in this Court to fullfil every article of our late treaty with expedition and exactness. Y. Lp. in your letter of the 11th ultimo mentions a desire of having some Xebecks or row Gallies. They have six such employ'd at present on the coasts of the Two Sicilies.... They have each a 24 Pounder on their bow, and upwards of One Hundred Men. Y. Lp.'s Letter dated from the Gulph of Genoa August 13th I received by the Post from Genoa, and not by Captain Inglefield, who is not yet arrived here. Having communicated the contents of this Letter also to General Acton, two of H.S.M.'s frigates were ordered to be got ready for service, and are actually in perfect readiness in this Port, to put themselves under the command of Captain Inglefield. Y. Lp. need not fear any disputes with respect to rank. Whatever Y. Lp. shall please to direct, H.S.M.'s Officers have orders to obey. It wou'd not be so with the Spaniards (as Y. Lp. may perhaps know) that the harmony between the Courts of Madrid and Naples is not yet perfect. This Court looks upon our late Treaty as meerly between Great Britain and the Two Sicilies, and that their stipulated Land and Sea Forces are only bound to act in the Common Cause, under Y. Lp.'s direction. Captain Cunningham in H.M.'s Sloop 'Speedy' arrived here a few days ago from Gibraltar, and I prevail'd upon him to stay a day or two longer than he intended in hopes that the two Xebecks mentioned in the former part of my letter might return and accompany him to the Fleet. On Sunday last I received the ratification of our Treaty which is now complete and in full force, and as Y. Lp. will see in General Acton's billet inclosed, this Court is only waiting the return of it's Consul from Marseilles to send off the Minister of the French Republic, to cut off all communication with France, and publish the Treaty.

ELPHINSTONE TO HOOD.

La Malgue, September 4.

I beg leave to present Y. Lp. a pair of Colours taken at Ollioules on 30th in testimony (tho' small) of the obligations I consider myself under in many instances to Y. Lp. I intended to have sent the other pair but some one has kept them in the Barrack.

SAME TO SAME.

La Malgue, September 4, 10 o'clock.

I have the honour to enclose Y. Lp. the report from Pharon; it is so scandalous that in my opinion Adm. Goodall ought to have it read *at* the whole Garde National to try if they have any sense of shame remaining; our troops could not restrain them such was their fear. I have two men from La Valette, where there are none of the enemy; they went on to the house of Madame Tilly and found about 40 posted there with a flesh [*flêche*] across the road and 2 small guns: this place is 2 miles farther than La Valette. Anything of note shall be duely communicated to Y. Lp.

MULGRAVE TO HOOD.

Toulon, September 8.

Having according to Y. Lp.'s directions taken upon myself the command of the British troops in Toulon; I have enquired, as far as the time would admit, into the strength and duties of the garrison. The line of defence is now contracted as much as it can be, consistently with the security of the Place, and I am in hopes that we have no reason to apprehend any serious impression from the present force of the Enemy; but from the circumstances which took place yesterday evening when the advanced Corps (which I had requested the Spanish Gen. yesterday morning to withdraw) were driven in, Y. Lp. will feel the absolute necessity of a reinforcement of *British* Troops. Should any Sickness take Place in consequence of the present hard duty; or any considerable disaffection appear amongst the inhabitants, our situation would become very precarious indeed; I beg leave therefore to submit to Y. Lp. the necessity of making an urgent requisition to Sir Robt. Boyd for a reinforcement of two battalions of infantry, with as large a detachment of artillery men, as he can spare from the necessary duties of his garrison (for we have not one Artillery man in the Garrison except a few Gunners from the Spanish Ships). I wish also to have an officer of Engineers. I should hope that the undoubted security of Gibraltar might enable the Governor so to reduce the duties, as to obviate any inconvenience to the garrison, from the above diminution of its numbers which I wish Y. Lp. to request for the safety of this most important Post. As the corps under my command are without their field officers, it will be desirable, if other considerations do not interfere, that the regiments detached to reinforce us, should be those which have the greatest proportion of field officers either regimental or by brevet. I shall without delay make every necessary regulation, for the regular and exact performance of the garrison duty at Toulon, and for the preservation of the health of the British troops upon whom our security so seriously depends.

HOOD TO COMMODORE LINZEE.

(Secret and Confidential.)

'Victory,' September 8.

You are hereby required and directed to proceed with the squadron under your command off the harbour of Villafranca and send a flag of truce on shore, with the letter you will herewith receive for the Senior captain of the French ships there, waiting off the port 24 hours for an answer; the purport of which you are to request may be addressed to you as well as to Adm. Trogoff, sending at the same time a number of the proclamations of amnesty, which you will send also to Oneglia by a frigate while you are waiting off Villafranca; and you will make known to the captains of the French ships there, that the harbour of Toulon, with every fort, is fully and completely possessed by me in trust for Louis XVII...until peace shall be restored.

[He will then proceed to Corsica, blockade the French garrisons in Bastia, S. Fiorenzo and Calvi, and after that, if they yield up those places to Paoli, and take the oath of allegiance to Louis XVII, they shall be conveyed to France on British vessels. Captain Masseria, a Corsican receiving his pay from England, and a confidential friend of General Paoli, will proceed with him. If these offers are refused, he will attack or seek to reduce by blockade the French garrisons.]

ACTON TO HOOD.

Naples, ce 12 Sept^{re}.

Informs him that "Sa Majesté Sicilienne voulait que le contingent qu'elle a promis de fournir, n'agisse pas sous d'autres ordres que ceux de V. Ex. et des autres Commandans de Sa Maj. Britannique. Elle peut donc ajouter pleine foy à tout ce que Le Maréchal [Forteguerri] aura l'honneur de lui dire, et je la prie de se communiquer à lui entièrement pour tout ce qu'elle jugera à propos et convenable d'être executé de notre part. Je puis d'ailleurs assurer V. Ex. que Sa Maj., exacte jusqu'au scrupule dans ses engagemens, a donné les ordres les plus précis, non seulement pour remplir ceux qu'elle a contracté[s] dans la Convention, mais pour se prêter au surplus en tout ce qui pourra dependre d'elle au dela du convenu. À mesure, que les autres vaisseaux seront prêts, on les fera partir de jour en jour pour rejoindre l'escadre, qui est sous ses ordres. Les ports des Deux Siciles, et tout ce que produisent ces royaumes sont de bien bon cœur offerts à V. Ex., pour tout ce qu'elle peut juger pouvoir être de quelque utilité ou satisfaction à V. Ex. à sa Flotte, et à tous les braves officiers qu'elle commande.

HOOD TO P. STEPHENS.

'Victory,' off Toulon, September 13.

I have the honour to acquaint you for the information of the Lords Comms. of the Admy. that, altho' we are kept in constant alarm by Carteaux's army in the West, and that of Piedmont in the East, each said to consist of from 5 to 6000 men, *such* as they *are*, I am under no apprehension of their being able to make any impression upon us. I am more afraid of an enemy within than without, and am therefore anxious to send off about 5000 turbulent disaffected seamen, which I hope to effect in 48 hours, as the ships are nearly ready for them; for should a serious attack be made, every one of them would take an active part against us as far as they could. I have the honour to enclose a Proclamation Don Langara and I have thought proper to issue and which we think will do much good.

'Victory,' off Toulon, September 14.

Copy of form of safe conduct for officer commanding each of the 4 ships destined to transport seamen from Toulon to their respective places of abode. Request that the ship be allowed to pass unmolested to the port designated, but if it be found straying from the direct course and cannot give justifiable reasons, the ship is to be detained with the crew as prisoners of war. Directed to all Admirals etc. of H.B.M.'s ships and to those of nations in amity with Great Britain at war with France.

Issued to 'Apollon' for Rochefort, 'Orion' for L'Orient, and to 'Patriote' and 'Entreprenant' for Brest.

DRAFT FROM LORDS COMMISSIONERS TO HOOD.

Whitehall, September 14.

Enclose for him, under flying seal, a letter to Sir Rob. Boyd, Governor of Gibraltar, in the supposition that he may find it necessary to have recourse to that garrison for the assistance of troops in the present emergency.

HOOD TO P. STEPHENS.

'Victory,' Outer Road of Toulon, September 14.

[Announces despatch of the four French ships, which was very necessary.]

The French do not want either ships or men, but stores of every sort they are most distressed for, and the greatest number of ships they could possibly equip either at Toulon or Brest, even by stripping all the remaining ones of masts, yards and cordage, is 23 or 24, and if the fleet at either port should be disastered by a partial action or a gale of wind, it could not put to sea a second time; this I have ocular proof of by examining the Arsenal here, and Admiral Trogoff assures me they are not better off at Brest, which place he left in October last. Being greatly distressed for money in my present situation for the service of the fleet under my command, I have sent the 'Romulus' to Naples for 20,000 $l.$

(Enclosure.)

State of the Troops on board Lord Hood's Fleet, September 14.

(Soldiers are not distinguished from marines.)

Soldiers and marines on board Lord Hood's fleet agreeably to the last returns.

Captains 15; First Lieutenants 21; Second Lieutenants 20; Sergeants 56; Corporals 62; Drummers 31; Privates 1421. Total 1626: of which there are in frigates 365.

First rates carrying 113—2; Second rates carrying 103—3, 102—1; Third rates carrying 80—1, 79—4, 62—1, 57—1, 56—1; without troops—7; Fourth ('Romney') carrying 48—1 = 22 sail. 14 frigates. 8 sloops, store ships etc.

(Sick on board 20. Sick on shore 30.)

KING FERDINAND TO HOOD.

Naples, 15 Sept^{re}.

Reçevés les Complimens sincères, et empressées, que je me fais un plaisir de vous addresser sur la reddition de Toulon. Le service important que vous venés de rendre à la cause comune, et surtout à l'Italie entiere, n'est dû qu'aux soins infatigables, et energiques que vous aves employés; il vous donne Milord un titre inefaçable a notre reconoissance. Je partage ce sentiment avec tous ceux qui vous le doivent si justement, mais éprouve une particulière satisfaction à vous temoigner combien il me penètre. Je fais exercer Milord tous les moyens, que la promptitude, et les circostances permettent d'employer pour concourir aux souhaits que vous aves fait parvenir a ma connoissance: il sera consolant pour moy de pouvoir au moins vous aider à conserver une aussy belle acquisition, et à en tirer le parti que le bien general va devoir a vos Soins, vos vues, et votre experience. La division de marine, et de troupes que je suis empressée de voir sous vos ordres tachera Milord, de meriter votre aprobation, ils sont flattés de suivre la carriere glorieuse où vous les introduirés, sous un aussy digne chef. Puissent vos succes être bientot couronnés par l'accomplissement des vœux que nous formons tous pour le bien, et la tranquillite generale? Je desire que les circostances me procurent la satisfaction Milord de vous assurer de vive voix de l'estime, et de la confiance, que vous m'aves inspirée.

DRAFT FROM LANGARA TO HOOD.

(Probably September 16.)

As I think we cannot show too great attention to Admiral Trogoff, whose conduct has been so perfectly correct, and full of zeal in the cause of monarchy which we mutually support, I think it is expedient and proper, that he should keep three ships of the line and three frigates, with half their complements of men, to be commanded by such Captains as he can rely upon on board in the Road, and that all the rest, who are to be cautious how men are, should be immediately carried into the bason, entered not well affected to the good cause and paid off. This will convey our perfect confidence in the admiral and our desire of looking upon all Frenchmen as friends, who manifest a desire of proving their duty, loyalty and attachment to Lewis the 17th. If this meets Y. Ex.'s approbation, as I trust it will, it will make me very happy and give a proof to the world of the liberality of our minds.

HOOD TO LANGARA.

September 16 and 17.

Conformable to what Y. Ex. has suggested respecting Admiral Trogoff, I most readily enclose a letter for Lord St Helens, which I entreat you will do me the honour to forward in Y. Ex.'s next dispatch, and am confident H. Lp. will be much pleased, indeed it is impossible he should not, for many reasons. In my last dispatch to my court, which leaves me to do whatever I shall judge right as circumstances arise, I made known my intention of shewing every mark of regard and esteem to the French Admiral that was in my power which he had a strong claim to; and that I proposed to allow him to have three ships of the line and three frigates in the Road in a state for Sea, that I should not hesitate occasionally to join a French ship, with two or three English ones, upon any service, and that I thought it a very right and prudent measure, on many accounts being persuaded much good would arise from it, and have not a doubt, of H.M.'s and His Ministers' full approbation of what I have proposed, as not a moment is to be lost to conciliate, and give accommodation where it can with propriety be done.

LORD HERVEY TO HOOD.

Leghorn, September 18.

This letter will be delivered to Y. Lp. by Mr Branzon, unto whom Captain Young[1] has been so good [as] to give a passage, that he may lay before Y. Lp. a statement of all the difficulties he meets with, and the total impossibility of his executing the orders he receives from Toulon; having tried every means in my power to have the sequestered corn given up, and finding my efforts useless, I do not see what step can be so proper as his going to relate the affair, get papers to prove the property to belong to the municipality of Toulon, and then return with fresh orders, as well as with new means: I hope Y. Lp. will approve of it, and cause him to be sent back here when his affairs are arranged. I must do Mr Branzon the justice to say, I think he acts with zeal and propriety.

[1] Capt. William Young, of H.M.S. 'Fortitude' (74) (see p. 50).

HOOD TO FRANCIS DRAKE.

(Secret and Confidential.)

'Victory,' Road of Toulon, September 24.

Whereas a small vessel with my passport, sent from H.B.M.'s ship bearing my flag, with commissioners deputed to me from Marseilles and in the service of a part of France that did not acknowledge the power of the Convention and consequently not subject to the jurisdiction of the persons employed by that Convention, was seized by the 'Modeste,' French frigate, laying in the mole of Genoa, and all her letters and other papers taken away and carried to Mr Tilly, agent from the Convention at Paris, and detained, which audacious conduct the Genoese Government has, to my great astonishment declined to take proper and marked notice of; and, it not being the first time the Republic of Genoa has manifested a glaring and highly unbecoming partiality in favour of French regicides to the prejudice of our most gracious sovereign and country,—I can no longer refrain from making use of H.M.'s naval force entrusted to me, to check and put a stop to such unjustifiable conduct, and have therefore sent R. Adm. Gell with a squadron to Genoa to consult and communicate with Y. Ex.; and I must request Y. Ex. will be pleased immediately to make known to the Doge and Senate, that, unless Mr Tilly is ordered to depart the Genoese territories within twelve hours, the port of Genoa shall be blockaded, and not a ship or vessel suffered to go in or out; and, as the Republic has in such numberless instances departed from a fair and honourable neutrality, Y. Ex. will be pleased further to acquaint the Doge and Senate of the absolute necessity of their making an instant, candid, and explicit declaration whether they wish to be looked upon as friendly or hostile to Great Britain, as open and avowed enemies are infinitely more sufferable than false friends. I am not a petitioner for favour, but in the name of my sovereign I demand justice from the Republic of Genoa, and hope and trust it will not be denied. R. Adm. Gell has my orders to seize the 'Modeste,' French frigate, the moment he arrives.

DRAFT LETTER OF LORDS COMMISSIONERS TO HOOD.

Whitehall, September 25.

Royal confirmation of his proclamation to the people of Toulon. No time will be lost in assembling a respectable military force commanded by Maj. Gen. O'Hara, who is ordered to proceed without delay to Toulon and take command of the troops from Gibraltar and of all other forces collected for the defence of Toulon and its dependencies. A commission appointing O'Hara governor of Toulon is forwarded, to be delivered to him by Hood, on his arrival. No exertion will be omitted to supply a force sufficient to repel attacks; and meanwhile reliance is placed on the fleet. Hood is to cooperate heartily with the land forces, and, when no longer required to confine his exertions to that particular service, he will follow the spirit of his former instructions by cooperating with other Powers and in giving such aid in every other quarter as his discretion may suggest, always bearing in mind that no service can be more important than to impress all powers bordering upon the Mediterranean with a just sense of the aid and protection which the naval Power of Great Britain is able to afford them. A commission will be granted immediately to him and to Sir Gilbert Elliot and Maj. Gen. O'Hara (who will both proceed immediately to Toulon) together with instructions, to enable them to superintend the various civil concerns which may arise either in Toulon or in such other places and provinces of France as may be inclined to recur to H.M.'s protection....

DRAFT LETTER FROM LORDS COMMISSIONERS TO HOOD
(marked "separate").

Whitehall, September 25.

In addition to my other dispatch of this date I have H.M.'s commands separately to convey to Y. Lp. H.M.'s pleasure with respect to one point arising out of the passage in Y. Lp.'s Proclamation of the 28 Aug. which relates to the objects for the sake of which H.M. took up arms, and which seemed to convey that one of those objects in the outset of the War was the reestablishment of the French monarchy. The true ground of the war was to repeal an unjust and unprovoked aggression against H.M. and his Allies and the rest of Europe, which had been evidently threatened and endangered by the conduct of France. In pursuit of these objects and with a view to a secure and honourable peace H.M. felt that circumstances might arise in the progress of the War which might make it prudent and necessary to interfere in the internal affairs of France, and to assist in reestablishing some regular government in that country in order to facilitate the conclusion of peace on such terms as H.M. might properly accept. Such a necessity has grown more and more apparent and the events which have taken place at Toulon afforded an opening for such interference too favourable to be neglected. H.M. therefore highly approves of Y. Lp.'s conduct in availing yourself as you have done of such an opening. But it is to be considered as arising out of the circumstances and founded on the considerations which I have stated and not as making part of the object for which H.M. originally took up arms....

HOOD TO J. GELL, R. ADM. OF THE BLUE.

'Victory,' Toulon Road, September 26.

...He is to proceed forthwith to Genoa with the 'St George,' 'Bedford,' 'Captain,' 'Mermaid,' 'Tartar,' 'Speedy,' 'Conflagration,' 'L'Eclair,' 'Vulcan' and 'Alert,' and immediately seize the French frigate 'Modeste' and every other French ship in the port, and get Mr Drake to intimate that the French agent for the Convention must quit Genoese territories within twelve hours, and that he will blockade Genoa until satisfactory security is given that Genoa will in future show more respect to the British flag and not show the least countenance to our enemies. Drake will also invite an explicit declaration from the government as to whether they wish to be looked upon as friendly or hostile to Great Britain. If he brings them to reason he will proceed to Leghorn (leaving the frigates and small vessels between Genoa and Villa Franca to prevent grain etc. being carried to that port or Nice) and seize the French frigate 'Impérieuse.' He will then desire Lord Hervey, the king's minister to Tuscany, to inform him of the result of his remonstrances to the Grand Duke respecting the audacious action of Mr Delaflote in sequestrating the property of Messrs Branzon and Roux, requesting Lord Hervey to intimate to the Grand Duke that unless he orders Delaflote to quit Tuscany within twelve hours, Leghorn will be blockaded, and also to ask the Grand Duke to declare whether he wishes to be looked upon as friendly or hostile to Great Britain.

HOOD TO EVAN NEPEAN.

'Victory,' Toulon Road, September 26.

...We are kept in perpetual alarms and at very hard duty. Carteau has erected batteries with heavy guns at the head of the Harbour near the village La Seyne, which we have twice destroyed by our floating batteries, covered by the 'Aurora' French frigate (which I officered and manned) and the 'St George,' under the direction of R. Adm. Gell, whose ship could not be carried quite near enough for want of water, her lower deck guns however did execution. On the 20th another strong Battery with heavy guns was opened, from which they fired red hot balls and shells. The 'Aurora' and one of the gun boats were set on fire, but it was soon extinguished without much mischief. The gun boat had three of her guns rendered unserviceable. The other gun boat, each of which carries four 24 prs., had one gun disabled and was so shook by a shell that she sunk. They had above 40 men killed and wounded. I shall have others placed so soon as the wind moderates, which has blown a gale for three days and at times very strong indeed, for the enemy must be kept at a distance at all risques, untill troops arrive, which would have been here, I am pretty sure some days ago but for the strong westerly winds, as I believe part of the 6000 I demanded from Naples sailed about the 9th and previous to that date three line of battle ships were waiting off Oneglia for two or three battalions from the King of Sardinia, but when we shall see them now God knows, as I fear they are driven to a distance.

'Victory,' Toulon Road, September 27.

I have the honour to desire you will be pleased to acquaint the Lords Commrs. of the Admiralty that H.M.'s ships 'Bedford' and 'Leviathan' came in, in the night, from Oneglia, and brought 800 of the King of Sardinia's good experienced troops, that have been fighting since April upon the mountains of Piedmont, and this day the Marshal Fortguerri, Commodore of His Sicilian Majesty's ships, arrived with 2000 troops in two ships of the line, two frigates and two sloops from Naples, all in perfect health, although 11 days on their passage; 2000 more may be expected in two or three days and the remainder to complete the number stipulated in the Convention would be ready in about 20 days from the sailing of the first Division now arrived; consequently they may be reasonably expected within a fortnight, all which, as well as the ships, are wholly at my disposal, as the King of the Two Sicilies has informed me, in a very gracious letter of His Majesty's own handwriting.

We are now perfectly at our ease; hitherto we have been at very hard duty, not a day has passed without our being attacked from one quarter or another, but as yet no impression has been made upon us in any respect, and we have been able to keep the enemy at a distance. The army of Carteau to the Westward is from 7 to 8000 men and that of Poypé's to the Eastward from 5 to 6000 according to the accounts received from deserters. Both have encreased very much laterly, but we do not now fear any number. Three Batteries have been three times opened upon our gunboats (each of which carried four 24 pounders) and the ships that covered them under the command and direction of R. Adm. Gell. The guns of which have been as often dismounted, and the works totally destroyed with very great slaughter, as the deserters say. The loss on the part of His Majesty in seamen is 9 killed and 34 wounded, but that includes many by the bursting of one of the 'St George's' lower deck guns; the Spaniards have lost about one third of that number. The 'Colossus' has gone to Cagliari for a battalion, and I have 3 ships (exclusive of the 'Berwick') at Gibraltar in full hope Sir Robt Boyd will not hesitate to send the 1500 men including artillery I have applied for.

P.S. I am exceedingly concerned to acquaint you that word is just brought me that Lieut. Newenham of the 'Windsor Castle' died an hour since of the wound he received three days ago in the defence of the Fort committed to his charge. H.M. has lost a very promising young officer; his gallant defence of the fort does him infinite honour.

HOOD TO GEN. PAOLI.

'Victory,' Toulon Road, September 29.

Previous to my receiving the letter Y. Ex. did me the honor to write me on the 25th Aug. I had ordered a squadron to Corsica under the command of Commodore Linzee (with whom Capt. Masseria embarked) who had directions to give Y. Ex. all the aid he could consistent with the safety of H.M.'s ships. In my present situation and the advanced season I can do no more. Had Y. Ex. some months ago made known to me your specific wants, and at the same time have been equally specific respecting the advantages you proposed to Great Britain in return, I might possibly have found an opening since I came upon the coast of Provence to have driven the French out of the Island.

Capt. Masseria arrived in Leghorn in June and I was repeatedly told from various quarters that he was charged with a commission to me from Y. Ex., but I saw nothing of him until the 6th of this month nor did I ever receive a syllable from him, and when he came he produced no credentials from Y. Ex. but only a memorial of his own setting forth the state of the Island. I however despatched all the force I could spare in three days after he came.

LINZEE TO HOOD.

H.M.S. 'Alcide,' Gulf of S. Fiorenzo, October 1.

Describes the unsuccessful attack of 'Alcide,' 'Courageux,' and 'Ardent' on forts in that gulf. 'Courageux' and 'Ardent' suffered much from raking fire of town of S. Fiorenzo, which the Royalists had reported out of range. Losses 15 killed, 39 wounded. (See *London Gazette*, Nov. 10, 1793).

ELPHINSTONE TO HOOD.

La Malgue, October 1, 10.30 a.m.

I have not saluted[1] only because I had never heard a word of any such intention nor anything further than a letter from the Committee General containing their desire and Y. Lp.'s approbation—but this is of a piece with everything from Toulon from which place I have never been able to obtain even a reply to any letter, nothing but incorrect messages, and contradictions, to the distruction of the publick service; of all this after having long withheld I have of late been obliged to complain.

---

[1] *I.e.* the *fleur de lys*, which had just been hoisted in Toulon.

Mulgrave to Hood.

October 1, 8.15 p.m.

I am but this instant returned from the Heights of Faron—from which we have completely driven the enemy with less loss than might have been expected under so heavy a fire and with such disadvantages of ground—Genl. Gravina has been slightly wounded in the leg—we have two British officers slightly wounded, Capt. O'Dougherty, and Mr Carter of the Marines; a Sardinian officer is killed—the troops all behaved with the greatest spirit; and the Neapolitans distinguished themselves much: we have several men killed and wounded—I have not yet breakfasted.

Draft from Lords Commissioners to Hood.

Whitehall, October 1.

He is aware of the reinforcements for the garrison of Toulon from Gibraltar, which should soon arrive, and should be followed in ten or fourteen days by nearly 300 cavalry and a complete battalion of Infantry from England. Measures have also been taken to send nearly 4000 Hessian Infantry, which should be ready to leave Ostend in about a month's time. The convoying ships can, if absolutely necessary, proceed to Toulon, but it is desirable, owing to the requirements of trade, that they should be released at Gibraltar.

It will be prudent to provide for the event of the enemy capturing Toulon, however unlikely it may be to happen. From Capt. Masseria and other information from Corsica he will have ascertained how far he can be accommodated there. If he has to evacuate Toulon he will appreciate the necessity to place himself in such a central situation as to be able to afford protection to the trade, and to annoy the enemy whenever they should attempt to leave their Ports. This caution is not out of any apprehension as to the situation, but merely to draw attention to the necessity of taking every precaution. If he has to withdraw he will, of course, send immediate notice to Gibraltar of his intended destination and make all the necessary regulations for convoys for trade.

Hood to P. Stephens.

'Victory,' October 6 (rec. November 9).

I have the honor to desire you will be pleased to offer to the Lords Comms. of the Adm. my sincere congratulations on a very brilliant and complete victory, obtained over the enemy the 1st instant upon the Heights of Faron: the British and Piedmontese troops composed the column under Lord Mulgrave and led the way; but H. Lp. gives full credit to the spirit and exertion of the troops of every nation, and is loud in the praise of the Neapolitans, who greatly distinguished themselves.... The action was short but hot: the enemy had upon the heights from 1800 to 2000 men, the flower of the Eastern army, not a fourth part of which, we are well informed, ever returned to H.Q.; for what did not fall by the bullet or bayonet broke their necks in tumbling headlong over the precipices in their flight.... [He then refers to Gravina's wound, and to the arrival of 'Colossus' with 350 troops from Cagliari.]

SAME TO SAME.

'Victory,' Toulon Road, October 7 (rec. November 9).

I beg you will be pleased to acquaint the Lds. Comms. of the Admy. that for the safety of Toulon and the security of H.M.'s ships under my command against the enemy's getting hold of the heights with which the Road is surrounded, I was compelled to the necessity of employing a number of floating batteries with heavy cannon, gun-boats and galleys (one of the former was sunk by a shell and another beat to pieces by shot), and have able and trusty officers in them, which were mann'd from the different ships of the fleet; and, it being equally necessary that the governors of La Malgue and Toulon should have an efficient assistant as Lieut. Governor, to enable them the more effectually to discharge the several duties of their very important stations, surrounded as we were with internal enemies, I appointed Lieut. Edward Cooke of the 'Victory' and Lieut. Robert Pamplin of the 'Princess Royal' to those stations, first signing a commission for each as commander of a sloop for a day, which I also did to the several midshipmen I appointed to command the floating batteries, gun-boats and galleys,—the latter being unavoidable in the Bay of Hières after Captain Reeves had destroyed the several batteries that obstructed the navigation of it, which was absolutely necessary to keep open on various accounts; and having no frigates to cover the floating batteries and gunboats, I took some French ones (which I should have done even if I had had some, thinking it better that they should be sunk or beat to pieces than my own) which were also manned from the ships of the fleet; and I appointed Commanders and Lieutenants to them, all which appointments I flatter myself their Lp's will approve and confirm, as not one has been made that there was not an unavoidable necessity for.... There has been killed and wounded in the floating batteries and gunboats upwards of 80 men.

LINZEE TO HOOD.

'Alcide,' off C. Corse, October 7.

[Reports the grounding of the 'Courageux': she must be sent to port. Letters captured from a privateer showed the distress of the

French garrisons of Calvi, Bastia, and Florenza [*sic*] for money and food.] Should Y. Lp. persevere in your intention of having the above ports blocked up, it will be necessary to have 4 or 5 ships or vessels cruising on the coast for that purpose, and if a cruiser can be placed off Antibes, she will be of much service as the Corsican mail and supplies come from that port....An officer of the 'Alcide' who was sent on the heights to reconnoitre the enemy's post [at Fornili] reports that four breaches were made in the wall on the land side, some of which were capable of admitting five men abreast. I shall therefore leave Y. Lp. to judge of the behaviour of the Corsicans who (tho' amounting to 1500 men on one side and 240 on the other) never moved from their ground to storm the works....

HOOD TO EVAN NEPEAN.
'Victory,' Toulon Road, October 7 (rec. November 9).

Encloses copy of a letter of Commodore Linzee, which justifies his opinion of Gen. Paoli as a composition of art and deceit and not to be depended upon. The allies won a brilliant victory over the enemy on the 1st upon the heights of Faron, of which Lord Mulgrave has given a particular account to Mr Dundas. Almost blind with writing, having so many ministers etc. to correspond with.

HOOD TO P. STEPHENS.
'Victory,' Toulon Road, October 7 (rec. November 9).

[As there may be dearth of flour for the troops and inhabitants of Toulon, he urges the despatch of two victuallers laden with flour: they will run no risk in coming from Gibr.] The enemy has made many attempts to cut off the water from the mills, and have succeeded in part. I think three out of seven are effectually stopped.

SAME TO SAME.
'Victory,' Toulon Road, October 13 (rec. November 9).

The enemy has erected another battery about 200 yds. south of the one destroyed by our sortie of October 9: but it has yet done us little harm.

MULGRAVE TO HOOD.
Toulon, October 14.

The firing you have heard proceeded from the impetuosity of an advanced Guard or rather Patrole of 100 British which I sent out under Capt. Wemys of the 11th Regt. who were engaged with a considerable party of the enemy. I sent fifty Piedmontese chasseurs with Chevalier Revel to bring them off, but finding they advanced I went out with the British and most of the Piedmontese troops to their assistance; two companies of Piedmontese chasseurs, two companies of Spanish Grenadiers, and two companies of Neapolitan

Grenadiers pushed forward on the left in imitation of the Patrole on the right: as soon as the Patrole on the right were brought off I sent an hundred British an hundred Piedmontese and a Battalion of Neapolitans to the assistance of the Grenadier Patrole which they met on their return; there are 2 or 3 British and 2 or 3 Piedmontese killed and two officers of the latter wounded; the affectionate emulation of the British and Piedmontese brought on this affair which I by no means wished to engage. The whole of the troops behaved with infinite gallantry, but I did not wish to engage them too far without cannon or I make no doubt we might have routed Carteaux's Army completely.

MULGRAVE TO HOOD.

October 15 [endorsed Toulon, October 16, 4 a.m.].

The unfortunate skirmish at Cape Brun this morning has cost us three most valuable officers. It occurred to me that the only means of dislodging the enemy from thence without an attack that would be precarious, and a loss we could little afford, would be by some manoeuvre that should oblige the enemy to abandon the post they had gained, I determined therefore to march out and take possession of the height of Thouars above la Garde and of that village if the enemy were not so immediately aware of my intentions as to get there before me; the unfortunate circumstance of the Spaniards having the turn of being upon the right—by the sloth of their movements prevented our occupying both Posts, and obliged us to be contented with the mere advantage of dislodging the enemy from Cape Brun and La Garde, without the advantage of a decisive action, which we certainly shd. have obtained had the British and Piedmontese troops led the column; as it is, the enemy for the present have retired, with all their cannon and troops to the distance of Sollices[1] at least; and we have only lost 1 man killed and 2 wounded in a rencontre between one of our Patroles, and the rear guard of the enemy. I will converse with Y. Lp. on our Situation, but I much fear till we have absolute command in English hands, and good troops entirely at British disposal; that no real good effects can be produced by efforts of sortie.

MULGRAVE TO HOOD.

Toulon, October 21.

Capt. Haddon of the 11th Regt. who is appointed Deputy Paymaster Genl. of the troops will have the Honour of presenting this to Y. Lp. and will give a receipt for £2000 for payment of the British army and French battalion, and the necessary expences.

The troops continue to be very irregularly served with provisions; at Malbousquet they had the day before yesterday received no provisions for two days—the soldiers on the hill of Faron receive still

---

[1] Solliès, a village five kilometres north-east of La Valette.

short allowance notwithstanding all the representations I have made; the provisions delivery from the Town are bad, the meat stinking, and the bread full of maggots. I understand Y. Lp. has appointed a commissary for the delivery of provisions to the army; I hope he will reside at Toulon and have a magazine and office there to which applications may be made, there is much discontent amongst the troops on account of their provisions and I fear it may be followed with very considerable desertion if they are not soon satisfied.

HOOD TO P. STEPHENS.

'Victory,' Toulon Road, October 26.

I have received your letter of the 1st inst. wherein you have it in command from the Lds. Comms. of the Admy. to signify their direction to me to remove the soldiers of the 30th regiment; serving in lieu of marines, as part of the complements of the ships of my squadron named in the margin[1], into the 'St George,' and the two 74 gun ships, which, by Their Lp.'s order of the 24th of last month, I am directed to send with R. Adm. Gell to Gibraltar; and to supply the places of the soldiers so removed with the soldiers or marines serving on board the ships which I may send with the R. Adm. as above mentioned; and that it was Their Lp.s' further direction to me to cause the part of the 30th regiment serving on board the 'Alcide' (in lieu of marines) to be removed into the 'Leviathan'; and the party of the 11th regiment, serving in the last mentioned ship, to be transferred, (previous to my sending her to Gibraltar), as directed by Their Lp.'s order of the 28th of last month, to the 'Alcide,' to serve in their room. In return to which it is my duty to observe that I humbly apprehend Their Lp.'s were not aware of the state of H.M.'s squadron under my command, and of the very critical situation in which I stand, having every soldier and marine serving as part of the complements of the respective ships (including the frigates) with upwards of 1000 seamen doing duty on shore and lent to divers vessels. I was obliged to send to every port in the Italian and other States for provisions, as the town of Toulon has no flour and but a few days' biscuits; and three fourths of the seamen, soldiers and marines are upon the *outposts*, which would be in great danger of falling into the hands of the enemy, were they withdrawn, as the defence of those posts depends entirely upon the English. Both the 'Windsor Castle' and 'St George' went to sea 200 short of complement. I shall, however, obey Their Lp.s' commands by sending the four ships to Gibraltar, distressing as I fear it will prove; but they must go without a soldier or marine unless General O'Hara consents, when he arrives, to my withdrawing the 300 privates of the 30th regiment, as directed in your letter. I made known to Lord Mulgrave the orders I had received, and herewith transmit his answer for Their Lp.'s information.

[1] 'Princess Royal,' 'Robust,' 'Terrible.'

MULGRAVE TO HOOD.

Toulon, October 26.

I have just received Y. Lp.'s letter informing me that letters have come to you from the Lords Comms. of the Adm. to embark 300 private soldiers, with their officers, from the 30th regiment, to complete the complement of four ships of the line. I think it my duty to represent to Y. Lp. that the whole of the British troops retained in the town of Toulon does not amount to 200 men, officers' servants and musicians included, and that from the nature of the troops at the out Posts and the extent of those posts, especially since the occupation of the exposed Post of Cap le Brun, at which 104 British privates are stationed, I am of opinion that 300 British troops cannot be withdrawn from the defence of this place before the arrival of the reinforcements from Gibraltar without the utmost hazard of the loss of some important out Post, which must be left without British troops if the 30th Regiment should be withdrawn. The enemy are every day receiving reinforcements. I forbear to give my opinion beyond the period of the arrival of the Gibraltar troops, as Y. Lp. will then have recourse to the better judgment of Major Gen. O'Hara.

HOOD TO H. DUNDAS.

'Victory,' Toulon Road, October 27 (rec. November 15).

I have been honored with your letter of the 5th and conformable to your wishes therein expressed I shall do my best to have ships at Gibraltar to protect any troops or stores from thence to this port so that the convoy which conducts them thither may proceed back to England immediately. Provided we all do our duty I am under no apprehensions that the enemy can gett possession of Toulon, but I shall, notwithstanding, be prepared against it as far as I am able. With respect to Capt. Masseria you will e'er this know, by a communication I made to Mr Nepean some time since, that he is a man not to be depended on, and I believe his principles are not sound. If however an opportunity for my giving Gen. Paoli temporary relief should offer, so as to enable him to hold out through the winter, I shall not fail to avail myself, so far as circumstances will admit of it, and flatter myself I shall find no great difficulty in driving the French out of the Island in the spring; but I have received no one instruction about Corsica, and my sending a squadron thither was a spontaneous action of my own, without having done much good by it. Disaster befell the ships, but am happy to say not a very material one.

Whatever hard fortune I may experience I shall take good care of the commerce of Great Britain, as well as that of His Majesty's Allies; by providing it with sufficient convoy. I am most exceedingly embarrassed at an order I have received to detach R. Adm. Gell in the 'St George' with three ships of 74 guns to Gibraltar, to proceed from thence to another part of the world, which is a most distressing circumstance, and am very confident it could not have been sent had the Lords Comms. of the Adm. been aware of the state of H.M.'s squadron under my command and of the very critical situation I now stand in,.... [The next sentences are the same as those at the end of his letter of Oct. 26 to P. Stephens.] The Spaniards are bringing their whole Mediterranean fleet to this Port. Don Langara says he shall have 26 sail of the line here in a few days.

SAME TO SAME.

'Victory,' Toulon Road, October 27 (rec. November 15).

Forwards instructions given to R. Adm. Gell, who has been detached with a squadron to Genoa, and for another squadron sent to Leghorn, as he considers it better to have open and avowed enemies than undermining friends. The measures have proved effective as each of these states has sent away the French consuls and their Jacobin adherents[1], and the Grand Duke has ordered the sequestrated property to be restored, with free liberty to export it to Toulon. Further particulars will no doubt be sent to Lord Grenville by Mr Drake and Lord Hervey.

SAME TO SAME.

'Victory,' Toulon Road, October 27 (rec. November 15).

By Lord Hugh Conway on the 24th I have your letters of the 25th ult. and 1st inst., and in obedience to the King's commands I have made known to the people of Toulon H.M.'s determination to perform as far as circumstances will admit the engagements I came under with them by affording protection to their persons and security to their property and by aiding and assisting them in such other salutary arrangements as may answer the great and important objects which induced them to put themselves under H.M.'s protection. I have received the commission you sent me for Maj. Gen. O'Hara, which shall be delivered to him on his arrival. I have such confidence in the zeal and exertion of the force with which H.M. has entrusted me, that no inconvenience will, I hope, arise, until such a force can be collected to act upon a more enlarged scale. The possession of what we have got I have not the least doubt of, be the enemy's force what it may....

HOOD TO P. STEPHENS.

'Victory,' Toulon Road, October 27 (rec. November 15).

Has recd. the Admy. order of Sept. 24 for Gell to proceed to Gibraltar, "which I shall comply with so soon as he returns from

---

[1] Incorrect as regards Genoa.

Genoa, and I have sent for him. The only 74 now with me in a condition for sea is the 'Captain'; the 'Courageux' is preparing to be hove down in consequence of her having been on shore at Corsica, and the 'Robust' is without a mainmast and none made for her; but I expect the 'Fortitude,' 'Colossus' and 'Leviathan' every day from Leghorn."

HOOD TO H. DUNDAS.

'Victory,' Toulon Road, October 27 (rec. November 15).

Forwards a letter received from the Committee General, Toulon, in answer to his communication made in obedience to instructions contained in the letter of the 24th ult. Major Generals O'Hara and Dundas have now arrived, and the commission to be Governor general of Toulon has been delivered to the former.

THE COMMITTEE GENERAL, TOULON, TO LORD HOOD.

Acknowledge the receipt of a communication regarding the engagements taken with the inhabitants of Toulon, and H.M.'s protection for them, for which they will be eternally grateful. Express their gratitude for the measures taken to recover the corn etc. sequestrated at Genoa and Leghorn. The Grand Duke's declaration in favour of the cause is due to his efforts. They are persuaded that they will experience nothing but benefits from the Coalesced Powers and congratulate themselves on being under his protection.

(Sd.) Gaston Aubany, Vice President

Eustaches, T. Baras, Bertrand.

HOOD TO H. DUNDAS.

(Private.) October 28, 5 p.m.

Gen. O'Hara has just been with me and alarmed me much. He says our Posts are not tenable and that we are in a dangerous situation for want of troops that can be relied upon: and what is very unpleasant is the conduct of the Spaniards, who are striving for power here. I have apprised Lord St Helens of it and will not longer detain my messenger than to say that Lord Mulgrave will follow him in 48 hours.

SAME TO SAME.

(Private.)

'Victory,' Toulon Road, October 31 (rec. November 23).

Lord Mulgrave, whose departure from this place I lament most exceedingly, has the goodness to take charge of my letters, and to H. Lp. I beg to refer you to our situation here, which, from what Gen. O'Hara has reported to me is not a very pleasant one; but yet I do not despair of overcoming every difficulty.

SAME TO SAME.

'Victory,' Toulon Road, October 31.

Encloses letters that have passed between Admiral Langara and himself since his last of the 27th. In spite of the difference upon certain points, it has not made any sort of breach between them. The common cause will not suffer, as Admiral Gravina and Gen. O'Hara perfectly understand each other.

HOOD TO DRAKE.

'Victory,' Toulon Road, November 8.

I am much concerned to find that the Genoese Government continues blind to its own true interest. I am inclined to think that, had all negotiation been omitted and a peremptory message sent, on the arrival of R. Adm. Gell, to know with precision what it would or would not do in the first instance, it might have been better; not that I in any manner condemn the attempt of bringing the Republic to its senses by negotiation, because I still think it would have been more desirable to have accomplished what we wished by that mode than by any other.

O'HARA TO HOOD.

Toulon, November 11.

With reference to the departure of the 'St George' and three 74's, and the proposed withdrawal of 300 men of the 30th Regiment to serve on board them as marines, the impossibility of the measure will be fully set out in a memorandum he is preparing on the military position of the army.

SAME TO SAME.

Toulon, November 11.

I beg leave to submit to Y. Lp.'s most serious consideration the situation of the combined forces assembled at Toulon. On my arrival here from Gibraltar the 27th of last month with a reinforcement of about 750 men, including the Royal Artillery, I found the city of Toulon completely invested, the enemy's batteries opened against the essential outposts and the space we occupied much circumscribed from the advantages which the local situation afforded them, and which a considerable length of time had given them the opportunity of improving. Struck with the extent and multiplicity of objects to be provided for (which not only comprehend the defence of the town but the covering a very spacious harbour) I have been assiduously employed in examining the several points on which the important operation of our defences depends, and I observe a circumference of about 15 miles occupied, to endeavour to secure the combined fleets in the two Roads and to cover the town, dockyards and arsenal from a bombardment, a circumstance not completely effected, as the enemy can from our experience of their present range, reach the latter from their batteries.

The position having been taken up under many unfavourable circumstances, from the want of engineers etc. has naturally produced the consequences that several of the posts are very injudiciously fortified, our means of improving them very inadequate, and the maintaining of them subject to many disadvantages. For it must be observed that with the Posts of Cepet and Balaguier we can have no other but a water communication which is often interrupted for many days successively by bad weather, and the troops stationed in all our outposts (many of which are on high and bleak situations, affording no proper cover to the men) being in consequence of their fatiguing duty greatly exposed to the severity of the season which has produced much sickness, I have reason to apprehend that insurmountable difficulties will occur in maintaining these posts through a rigorous winter and particularly should the enemy be reinforced with the numbers we have reason to expect in consequence of the recent unfavourable change of affairs at Lyons.

Seven thousand men now occupy these outposts. That number will not ensure their safety, if they be vigorously attacked; and in this place I must beg leave to repeat that should we be able to maintain all these Posts, it may not prevent the dockyard and arsenal from being bombarded. Thus circumstanced the dislodging of the enemy can alone relieve us from our embarrassed situation. But after mature deliberation, with every intelligence that can be obtained, such a force as we can assemble is very far from ensuring the accomplishment of that object. For the nature of the country is such that it affords the enemy the greatest advantages. Being mountainous, laid out into terraces, covered with timber, intersected by deep rocky ravines and offering (to those points where any decisive impression can be made) no roads for artillery except the great one to Ollioules, for the defence of which they have particularly provided, and from corroborating intelligence the enemy have improved these natural advantages by intrenchments, abbatis etc., protected with a numerous artillery. If any attempt to dislodge the enemy should be unsuccessful, the town with all its dependencies, the combined and French fleets would be exposed to the most imminent danger.

From this view of our situation it is my decided opinion (in which I have Maj. Gen. Dundas' authority to say he fully agrees with me) that the security of Toulon and its harbour can only be secured by the position of an army in the field amply prepared for that service and necessarily covering a very considerable district of country. It is however essential that Y. Lp. should be apprised that, excepting the Neapolitans and a few of the British, the Spaniards and Sardinians are totally unprovided with artillery, tents, camp equipage and every article indispensible for taking the field at this late season.

And I must beg leave to submit, as an additional reason for delaying any attempt to dislodge the enemy from their present position, the waiting for the arrival of reinforcements of British and Austrian troops which I understand may be daily expected. And though it must also be taken into consideration that the quality and discipline of the greatest part of our present numbers give no very encouraging prospects in any attempts we may make, still the last resource to dislodge the enemy must be kept in view, whatever difficulties may attend the execution to be adopted, whenever circumstances may compel us to that necessity.

It may appear foreign to the immediate object of this letter, yet I must beg leave to add that from the intelligence I have been able to collect, as well as from my own observations no country is less calculated to subsist a large army, and in none can its progress be more easily impeded. How far these circumstances must give way to other considerations I am not enabled to judge. They are stated as military difficulties arising from our very peculiar situation. Thinking it my indispensible duty to lay before the king's ministers with every dispatch possible our very critical situation, I am to request Y. Lp. will have the goodness to afford me the means of making that communication.

HOOD TO H. DUNDAS.

'Victory,' Toulon Road, November 13 (rec. December 8).

Forwards two letters of Lt. Gen. O'Hara with all possible expedition. Governor O'Hara having enough to do in discharging his various duties in Toulon has desired that Capt. Elphinstone shall take care of the great fort of La Malgue, until some general officer arrives from England to put in charge of it.

HOOD TO P. MAGRA (British Consul at Tunis).

'Victory,' Toulon Road, November 19.

By Lord Amelius Beauclerk, Captain of H.M.S. 'Nemesis,' I re-ceiv'd your letters of the 31st of last month and the 10th instant. The one you say you wrote me on the 29 of September has never come to hand, so that I am unable to say a word upon the subject of it, whatever that might be; I am very sensible of the mischief that has arisen, by Captain Lumsdaine not delivering my letter to you of the 27th of June in his way to Tripoli[1], because that would have prevented the ill humour you have experienced from the Bey, by the artifice and knavery of the Jacobin French. [He then refers to the suspicious conduct of a Spanish Admiral at Tunis. He regrets the favour shown by the Bey to the French, but hopes he will imme-

---

[1] For this incident see Chapter II.

diately abandon a banditti of regicides.] The port of Genoa is blockaded by a part of the fleet under my command, so as to prevent the common Enemy from receiving supplies from that Republick. The coalesced sovereigns do not mean to meddle with the form of Government in France, their only desire is upon the principles that common humanity dictate to establish a permanent one and to give peace to Europe upon a solid basis, leaving wholly to the French whether it shall be monarchal or any other, and to satisfy the Bey upon this head, I have sent the Commodore a manifesto of the King of Great Britain's which he is desired to communicate to H. Ex.[1] But should the Bey after this be determined to countenance and protect the French regicides, it will be very painfull to our Royal Master, as H.M. is very desirous of cultivating and maintaining H. Ex.'s friendship. Much caution and circumspection is therefore necessary not to involve H.M.'s Subjects in difficulty. It will however be expedient you should suggest to the Bey, that it will be necessary for the support of the common cause in which the Coalesced Powers are united to use all the means in their power to prevent the French merchandize now at Tunis from being carried into France, by any circuitous channel, or artifice whatever. I have desired Commodore Linzee to remain at Tunis, as long as you shall judge his presence absolutely necessary for the countenance and protection of H.M.'s subjects in that Kingdom but no longer.... We can get no advantage by quarrelling with the Bey, and his friendship may be of use, if he will give it us heartily, which you must use all the persuasive means in your power to secure....

HOOD TO HAMILTON.

'Victory,' Toulon Road, November 21.

My little pacquet boat had rather a tedious passage from Naples. As I did not receive the very obliging letter Y. Ex. did me the honor to write me, on the 31st of last month, until the 15 instant at night, I am perfectly at a loss what the Chevr. Fortiguerri means by my receiving and treating him with great coolness from his first coming, because I am conscious of not having given occasion for his saying so in the least degree whatever. Upon his arrival, I requested the honor of his company and that of all his captains to dinner the next day, after that I called alongside his ship, but had not the good fortune to find him on board. I then met him (?) at dinner on board the 'Britannia,' the ship that bears V. Adm. Hotham's Flag, who is next in command to me; the second day from that I repeated my invitation to him to meet the flag officers of my fleet with Admiral Langara, but he was unluckily engaged; his captain however came and he did me the honor, a few days after that to ask me to dine with

[1] This must be the Royal Proclamation of October 19, 1793 (see *Ann. Reg.*, 1793).

him, I made a point of waiting upon him although I was at that time far from well, and it would have been better for me to have staid in my own Ship as I have ever since been almost wholly confined to my Cabin; The Chevr. therefore has shewn a great want of fairness, and candour for covering and attempting to justify his very extra-ordinary conduct; he is undoubtedly, the proudest most empty and self sufficient man, I ever had anything to do with, and totally ignorant of the common rudiments of Service. I am sorry to say he has most evidently proved himself. If the King of Naples intended, as I am very confident H.M. did by sending his Fleet, that it should be fully assisting to the good of the common Cause entrusted to me and not to gratify the pride and vanity of Commodore Fortiguerri (who is fond of having as many Neapolitan Flags daily to look at as he can), the captains must be under my orders or it is useless in a great measure: for instance if I should see occasion to send three or four Neapolitan Ships to Sea with three or four English, it would be impossible for Commodore Fortiguerri to give them orders because the officer under whose command they would be put would neither know where he was to go or what he was to do, until he was at some distance from the port. We have spies all round us employed by the Convention, and therefore *intended Services* for any part of the Fleet under my command must be perfectly secret.

[Hood then says that he does not interfere with the Neapolitan ships while in port, but they cannot go to sea without his orders. (For the paragraphs here omitted see *The Naval Miscellany* (N.R.S.), I, 239, 240.)]

...What the Chevr. can mean by saying that Y. Ex.'s Letters to Toulon have been the occasion of the Neapolitans being humbled as they are, I cannot guess, and think he ought to be called upon to explain himself. But it is rather singular that I should have a similar charge against me for being partial to the Neapolitans. I am afraid I must plead somewhat guilty to this if I am judged by my thoughts (but on no other account) because I do not hesitate to say that I have a far better opinion of the Sicilian troops than I have of the Spanish, but confined as I have been to my Ship for some time by bodily complaints it has not been in my power to shew partiality to either. Y. Ex. will I am sure allow that the Neapolitan troops have a claim to a preference in my estimation when I relate what passed in the evening of the 15th, between four and five o'clock. Our Post (and a very material one it is) upon the Heights of Grasse was attacked and would have been lost but for the presence of Lieutenant General O'Hara, Governor of Toulon, at a very critical moment; H. Ex. was very fortunately on board the 'Victory' to meet our colleague, Sir Gilbert Elliot, who arrived from Genoa in the preceding night, and on perceiving the firing to increase got into a boat and rowed for the shore as expeditiously as possible; when he reached the height the French were almost close to the work, the Spaniards retreating and firing their musquets in the air, upon which the Governor sent for the Royals to advance who jumped off the works and were soon followed by a dozen or fifteen Neapolitans, emulous of imitating so good an example under the eye of their General who could not bring the Spaniards forward, by which the enemy were put to flight. This is the report the Governor made to me on his return to the 'Victory' about eight o'clock. I herewith send Y. Ex. an account of the killed, wounded, and missing of the combined forces as made to me next morning; we know not the loss of the enemy but it must be pretty considerable as seventy musquets were collected with many dead bodies and some mortally wounded....

H. DUNDAS TO HOOD.

London, November 23.

Lord Mulgrave arrived a few hours ago and from the report he makes to me of the state of the garrison of Toulon it is impossible to be free from the alarm which Y. Lp. expresses in your letter, I this day received. Under these circumstances I am sure I need scarcely remind Y. Lp. of the propriety (in case of any disaster happening) of having the French ships captured at Toulon so situated that if you was obliged to abandon the place none of the ships or arsenals of Toulon should be permitted to fall into the hands of the enemy. The arsenals must be destroyed and the ships burnt if they cannot be carried with you. I hope they may be brought away, and in such circumstances as I have referred to this would be perfectly justifiable under the nicest and strictest interpretation of the terms of the agreement entered into by Y. Lp. with the people of Toulon[1].

ELLIOT TO HOOD.

Toulon, November 24.

I am extremely obliged to your Lieutenant for the Letters and other papers which Mr Fraser has delivered to me and which I now return. Y. Lp.'s answer to Admiral Langara No. 4 appears to me perfectly proper, and it does not occur to me that any addition should be made to it. If this correspondence should proceed further, perhaps it might be worth while to observe that in the present state of things we cannot with propriety oppose any party which acts against the Convention of France, but that it is politick, even for the interests of his Most Christian Majesty, that all the enemies of that body should be treated as friends by the combined Powers, reserving for future opportunities, the discussion of their pretensions.

I have been preparing despatches for the messenger Basilico, whom

---

[1] This letter fixes the date of Pitt's undated letter to Grenville in the *Dropmore P.*, II, 471, as November 23.

I presume Y. Lp. will think it proper to send to England, by the earliest opportunity. I have been a little delayed by an indisposition in my stomach and bowels, which has been pretty severe these two days, and has prevented me from paying my respects to Y. Lp., as I should otherwise have done. My despatches will be ready in an hour and I shall have the honour of communicating them to Y. Lp. in the course of the day. I have taken the liberty of writing one in the name of the Commissioners, which will require Y. Lp.'s signature, if you should approve of it. I have written another of greater length which, to avoid the inconvenience of formality, I have used the freedom to write in my own name; but which I shall also have the honour of submitting to Y. Lp.

There are many important and pressing points, in which it will be necessary to consult Y. Lp. in the course of a day or two, and I will take the first favourable moment to wait on you on board the 'Victory' for that purpose. I am extremely sorry to learn your indisposition, and I hope you will not think of coming on shore till you are perfectly recovered.

HOOD TO H. DUNDAS.
'Victory,' Toulon Road, November 24.

On information received from Mr Trevor and Mr Drake he sent V. Adm. Cosby to Vado Bay with sufficient tonnage to bring 5000 Austrian troops from Milan, who were to move to the coast on the 10th or 12th of last month. After his arrival V. Adm. Cosby was informed by Mr Drake that the troops must embark at Leghorn, as there were horses and mules for them, for which forage could not be procured in Genoese territories, and accordingly he went thither. By letters of the 18th from Mr Trevor Hood learns that there is not a shadow of hope left for seeing a single soldier at Toulon from Milan. This is a woefull disappointment.

SAME TO SAME.
'Victory,' Toulon Road, November 26 (rec. December 22).

Encloses some recent correspondence with Langara, in which he has opened the views of his Court more than he has ever done before, though Hood saw very plainly what they were.

ADM. LANGARA TO HOOD.
'Concepcion,' Toulon Road, November 20.

Notifies him of arrival in Toulon last night of a small vessel from Corsica, having neither the white colours nor the national. Considers that the coalesced Powers cannot look with indifference on an independency that will be an usurpation of the Island of Corsica. Hopes to have his opinion with regard to ordering them to hoist the white colours and letting the islanders know that they must not use any others. Anxious to coincide in his ideas, as his sovereign wishes them to agree in everything.

HOOD TO ADM. LANGARA.

Acknowledgement. Always understood that a very great part of the inhabitants of Corsica refused to acknowledge themselves subjects of France; so does not see upon what ground he can prevent vessels coming from a part of the island (not belonging to or in possession of the French) from wearing the Corsican flag as this port is *at present* virtually English.

ADM. LANGARA TO HOOD.
'Concepcion,' Toulon Road, November 23.

In his letter of the 21st observes the expression that the Port is at present virtually English. Thinks it incumbent upon him to state that he considers and holds it as delivered in deposit to Spain and England, who have concurred equally with all their force to preserve it for the legitimate sovereign, Louis XVII. For that effect the squadrons entered the Port at the same time, and Spanish troops were sent immediately after, who prevented the place from falling into the enemy's hands. With this view and having always acquiesced in every important matter that has happened since their arrival, he requests H. Ex.'s sentiments with respect to the colours of the Corsican vessel.

HOOD TO ADM. LANGARA.
'Victory,' Toulon Road, November 24.

Very sensible of the opportune assistance rendered by H. Ex. in maintaining possession of Toulon. Begs him not to discuss points which their Courts only can settle. Considers that the Corsicans, who have never acknowledged themselves subjects of France, have the right to use the Corsican flag.

HOOD TO H. DUNDAS.
'Victory,' Toulon Road, November 30 (rec. December 24).

The enemy having erected and opened a battery against the Post of Malbousky and from which shells would reach the town and Arsenal, Governor O'Hara signified to me yesterday his intention to attempt to destroy it and bring off the guns and requested some sea-men to be sent to a post he proposed to withdraw British soldiers from. The governor promised not to go out himself, but unfortunately did not keep his word. A most clear, distinct and regular plan was settled and the commanding officer of the Troops of each Nation had a copy of it. The troops moved at 4 o'clock this morning and surprised the Redoubt most completely. Never was a service performed with more regularity and exactness, but the ardour and impetuosity of the Troops (instead of forming on the heights where the battery was raised, as they were particularly ordered to do) led them to rush like so many foxhounds after the enemy near a mile on the other side in a very scattered and irregular manner. The consequence of which was the enemy collected in very great force, and in the retreat of our troops they suffered very extremely. I herewith transmit an account of the loss of the British in killed and wounded and missing, but Major Gen. Dundas will give you more particulars. The Governor most unfortunately was wounded and taken prisoner; a surgeon was sent to him immediately (by permission of Gen. Du Gommier, Commander in Chief of the Eastern Army at the siege of Toulon) who reports that the governor's wound is a flesh wound only in the arm, but being faint by the loss of blood was obliged to sit down under a wall and there made prisoner of.

(Enclosure.)

List of British Casualties.

Lt. Gen. O'Hara wounded and taken prisoner; 2 officers, 18 men killed; 5 officers 78 men wounded; one officer wounded and missing; 2 officers wounded and prisoners; 88 men missing.

SAME TO SAME.

'Victory,' Toulon Road, December 1 (rec. December 24).

Transmits extract from letter just received from V. Adm. Cosby respecting the loss of the French ship 'Scipion' on Nov. 26 in Leghorn Road. Has authorised R. Adm. Trogoff to hold an enquiry.

DRAKE TO HOOD.

Leghorn, December 13.

[He is concerned that Lord Hood disapproves his conduct at Genoa: but the state of things there differed greatly from that at Leghorn: at Genoa there was a French army near the frontier, and the Genoese had much money in the French funds, the Jacobins also being very powerful in Genoa. Further the Genoese authorities ordered their forts to fire on H.M.'s ships if they sought to take 'la Modeste' out of the Mole—an order set aside 5 days later on his (Drake's) representations.] ...An immediate and peremptory message would have strengthened rather than weakened the Jacobin party; and indeed many of those who were at first violent against us were in the sequel brought to think differently. [He thinks it was impossible to succeed, the Jacobins being too strong.]

HOOD TO H. DUNDAS.

'Victory,' Toulon Road, December 13

(rec. January 13, 1794).

Nothing very material has happened here since the 30th of last month, when I had the honour of writing to you, except that the enemy has made approaches nearer to us by some new-erected batteries—one against Malbousquet, another against Le Brun, and a third against the Hauteur de Grasse. The shells from two of them did us some mischief on the 9th and 10th, since which they have been perfectly silent. The enemy is reported to be 50,000, but I cannot credit their being much beyond half that number, by various deserters that have come in, which in this respect perfectly agree, we are soon to be attacked on all sides at once. The arrival of Sir James Erskine St Clair has damped our spirits, as he reports we have no expectation of succours beyond his regiment of 300 men. This is certainly melancholy news: yet I do not despond. We are, however, from the numerous and important Posts we have to occupy, at very hard duty, and without relief some way or other, we shall soon have more men in the Hospitals than are fit for service.

ADMIRALTY TO HOOD.

(Secret.)

London, December 20.

Acknowledge receipt of letter of 13 Nov. enclosing Gen. O'Hara's account of the critical position of the troops at Toulon. A similar letter received from Gen. O'Hara. Hope there is no need for alarm for the safety of Toulon as Gen. O'Hara's letter would suggest, if unaccompanied by other considerations. However it is expedient to be thoroughly prepared. The fleet and the preservation of H.M.'s troops at Toulon must be his first care. Scarcely less important, in the improbable event of his being obliged to abandon the place, is to provide so far as circumstances will admit for the safe removal of as many as possible of the well affected inhabitants. A third object is to render the place, when no longer tenable, of as little value as possible to the enemy, particularly by the destruction of the Arsenals.

With regard to the disposal of the French ships in the harbour the Toulonese must agree that the worst of all possible events and the one most incompatible with the spirit of the agreement with them would be the reversion of those ships to the power of the National Convention, and in such a prospect they would heartily concur in totally destroying them except such as may be needed as transports to remove the inhabitants. Gibraltar would be the best place to take them to, if practicable, except English ports, and after that, Naples or any other friendly ports in the neighbourhood. If necessary there would presumably be no difficulty in arranging with the Spaniards for a part to be lodged in some of the Spanish ports. This would probably facilitate the execution of the measure, as it is known that the Spanish Admirals have received instructions, in the event of the abandonment of the place, to concert the removal with Lord Hood; and the Spanish government have expressed the wish that the whole should be removed to their ports. Such a proposition is, for many obvious reasons, totally inadmissible, but if removal becomes necessary and practicable, there would be no objection to the Spaniards sharing in the removal and custody of such a proportion of the ships as Lord Hood might think expedient under the circumstances of the moment. But in such case a written declaration must be given by the Spanish Admiral, expressly declaring that this measure is taken only as a matter of necessity, and with a view to the provisional custody of the French ships, which the Court of Spain must become bound to restore to France when by the establishment of monarchy and the restoration of peace, on the footing of the agreement made with the Toulonese, and it must also be part of the agreement that they are not to be restored without the consent of the British government in any other event. He will communicate the contents of this letter to Gen. O'Hara, who will be directed to cooperate with him in the execution of such measures as may be necessary in the very improbable event, it is hoped, which has given rise to these instructions.

SAME TO SAME.

Whitehall, December 28.

Maj. Gen. Dundas will have communicated to him what was written about the Austrian troops ordered from the Milanese, and Hood should concert with him the means most advisable for obtaining the services of these troops at Toulon in the speediest manner.

HOOD TO H. DUNDAS.

'Victory,' Hières Bay, December 20

(rec. January 15, 1794).

I am much distressed that it is my duty to acquaint you that I have been obliged to evacuate Toulon, and to retire from the harbour to this anchorage. Fort Mulgrave, upon the heights of Grasse, was attacked on the north part of the Spanish lines at two in the morning on the 17th, the enemy having kept up a continual discharge of shot and shells for 24 hours before. There was an appearance at a distance that the post was well defended; but it seems the right occupied by the Spaniards gave way, by which the enemy entered the works and soon got full possession of the height. The enemy declined to follow the combined Troops, who retreated to the next hill, and, having destroyed a great part of the fort they had taken possession of, retired for a considerable time; but, there being a want of spirit and vigour to attempt to retake the Post, the enemy took courage and in the afternoon came on again in great force, which occasioned a total evacuation of all the heights and a retreat to the boats.

Very early in the morning Don Lángara came to me and expressed great impatience for a council of all the principal officers of navy and army to be called, at which, late in the afternoon it was decided to retire at a fixed time after proper regulations were made for it. But on that very night the whole of the Neapolitans stole off from the town without the consent or knowledge of the governor, and a letter having been received at the council from Captain Elphinstone addressed to the governor, informing him that the Neapolitan Colonel, commanding upon Cape Brun had in express terms said he would not defend the post if it was attacked, but would retire with all his men; and a similar report having been made to the Governor next morning that the Commanding officer of the Neapolitans upon the post of Sepet had declared he would remain on it no longer, it became unavoidably necessary that the retreat should not be defer'd beyond that night, as the enemy commanded the town and ships by their shot and shells. I therefore, agreeable to the Governor's plan, directed the boats of the fleet to assemble by 11 o'clock near Fort La Malgue, and am happy to say the whole of the troops were brought off to the number of near 8000 without the loss of a man; and in the execution of this service I have infinite pleasure in acknowledging, because it is my duty to do so, my very great obligation to Captain Elphinstone for his unremitting zeal and exertion, who saw the last man off, and it is a very comfortable satisfaction to me that several thousand of the meritorious inhabitants of Toulon were sheltered in H.M.'s ships. I propose sending the V. Adms. Hotham and Cosby with some other ships to Leghorn or Porto Ferrara [Ferrajo] to complete their wine and provisions, which run very short, having many mouths to feed, and to remain with the rest to block up the ports of Toulon and Marseilles. The [unaccountable panic that has taken hold[1]] of the Neapolitan troops made the retreat absolutely necessary to be effected as soon as possible, and prevented the execution of a settled arrangement for destroying the French ships and arsenal. I ordered the 'Vulcan' fireship to be primed, and Sir Sidney Smith, who joined me from Smyrna about a fortnight ago, having offered his services to burn the ships, I put Captain Hare under his orders, with the Lieuts. Tupper and Gore of the 'Victory,' Lieut. Pater of the 'Britannia,' and Lieut. R. W. Miller of the 'Windsor Castle.' Ten of the enemy's ships of the line in the Arsenal, with the masthouse, great storehouse, hemp-house and other buildings were totally destroyed, and before daylight all H.M.'s ships, with those of Spain and the Two Sicilies were out of the reach of the enemy's shot and shells, except the 'Robust' which was to receive Capt. Elphinstone, and she followed very soon after without a shot striking her.

[1] These words are pencilled out and the word "conduct" in pencil is substituted.

I have under my orders R. Adm. Trogoff in the 'Commerce de Marseilles,' 'Puissant,' and 'Pompée,' of the Line; the 'Pearl,' 'Arethusa,' and 'Topaz' frigates, and several large corvettes which I have mann'd and employed in collecting wine and provisions in the different ports in Spain and Italy, having been constantly in want of one species or another, and are now at short allowance.

Don Langara undertook to destroy the ships in the Basin, but I am informed found it not practicable; and as the Spanish troops had the guarding the powder vessels which contained the powder of the ships I ordered into the Basin and arsenal on my coming here, as well as that from the distant Magazines within the enemy's reach, I requested the Spanish Admiral would be pleased to give orders for their being scuttled and sunk; but, instead of doing that, the officer to whom that duty was entrusted blew them up, by which two fine gun boats which I had ordered to attend Sir Sidney Smith were shook to pieces. The lieutenant commanding one of them was killed and several seamen badly wounded. I am sorry to add that Lieut. Goddard, of the 'Victory,' who commanded the seamen on the heights of Grasse, was wounded but I hope and trust not dangerously.

I beg to refer you for further particulars to General Dundas respecting the evacuation of Toulon, and to Sir Sidney Smith as to the burning of the enemy's ships, &c., on which service he very much distinguished himself: and he gives great praise to Capt. Hare of the fireship, as well as to all the lieutenants employed under him. It is with very peculiar satisfaction I have the honor to acquaint you that the utmost harmony and most cordial understanding has happily subsisted in H.M.'s army and fleet, not only between the officers of all ranks, but between the seamen and soldiers also....

Abstract of the Return of Killed, wounded and missing on the 17th day of December 1793, at Fort Mulgrave.

	Killed	Wounded	Missing	Total
'Victory'	—	4	8	12
'Britannia'	8	—	—	8
'Windsor Castle'	2	2	2	6
'Princess Royal'	—	—	9	9

Lieut. Goddard and Midshipman Loring of the 'Victory' wounded. Midshipman A. Wilkie of the 'Princess Royal' missing.

SAME TO SAME.

'Victory,' Hières Bay, January, 1794
(rec. February 18, 1794).

By the messenger Dressing I had the honor to receive on the 19th at night your secret letter of the 20th of last month; and, as you will e'er [sic] this be informed that H.M.'s ships and troops have been obliged to retire from Toulon, it is perfectly unnecessary for me to trouble you much upon the subject of your Instructions; but I hope and trust H.M. will be fully satisfied that I did as much mischief to the enemy's ships and the arsenal of Toulon as the circumstances would permit, and that every inhabitant was brought off as manifested inclination to come; but I most earnestly wish more had done so, from the insatiable revenge that has been taken. A few days ago a small Tartane came here from a little place between Toulon and Marseilles with seven unfortunate refugees on board to claim my protection, every one of which has been examined, and I herewith transmit what the most intelligent of them has declared, confirmed in general by the whole.

With respect to the removal of the French ships, it was by no means practicable in the state they lay in the arsenal and bason totally dismantled: it would have taken a very considerable time to have put them in a situation and proceed to sea, if I could have furnished men to have done it, which would have been extremely difficult from the great number of seamen (exclusive of the troops which were embarked as part of the ships' complements in lieu of Marines) I had ordered on shore upon various services; but, admitting that to have been practicable, it would have been totally impossible to have found men to have navigated them, for the complement of every ship under my command was so reduced by sickness and in killed and wounded that I was under the necessity of having recourse to the Grand Master of Malta for the loan of 1000 men to serve in H.M.'s fleet, which His Eminence immediately and in the handsomest manner granted, 400 of which arrived since I anchored in this bay, and I hourly expect the remainder by the 'Captain' (whose commander I sent upon the service) and 'Aurora,' French frigate, which I put a few men on board of for the purpose, and I was obliged to take the Marines from every frigate to put on shore. I however cannot help thinking that it was far better to destroy the French ships than to bring them away, even if it could have been done with most perfect convenience; and, had the Spanish Admiral fulfilled what he engaged to do, the whole would have been burned; but I am not now surprised at Don Langara's conduct, as he told a very respectable person (who does not hesitate to declare it) that it might be for the interest of England to burn the French fleet, but that it was by no means the interest of Spain. I am detained here very much against my wishes and inclinations, for want of bread and wine, which we are much distressed for: I have been in hourly expectation of the former by the convoy from Gibraltar for a fortnight past (R. Adm. Gell having informed me it would certainly sail on the 24th of last month) and of the latter from Alicante and Port Mahon, as I sent vessels for it six weeks ago. [Sir Hyde Parker for reasons of health will quit the position of Hood's first Captain and will hoist his flag on the 'Bedford,' and on the 'St George,' when it is possible.]

APPENDIX F

CONFIDENTIAL LETTERS FROM LORD MULGRAVE TO PITT AND DUNDAS

(Private.)

Toulon, September 15 (rec. October 4).

Dear Pitt,

In addition to my official correspondence I think it a duty of friendship to give you a particular assurance of the confidence I feel of the safety of this place, unless the troops should misbehave in a most disgraceful and improbable manner at the outposts; if we were even to lose them, the enemy could not get possession of the town except our enemies within should be bold and enterprising and those who have called us hither should be afraid to stand by us; and even in that worst event I have concerted measures for securing a retreat and for burning the Arsenal and dockyard; but these are vague and I think improbable suppositions. I fear no enemy but the sickness or fatigue of the troops. I therefore make every effort to provide good covering for them before the rains come on; and I rather delay strengthening our defences than employ the soldiers in any labour, for it would be truly *propter vitam vivendi perdere causas* to break an army by erecting works for them to defend.

Don Gravina, the Spanish Admiral commanding the troops on shore, is the great favourite of the King of Spain: I find him the most zealous and practicable man with whom I ever had any transaction. He is not jealous of command, and has opposed no one proposal I have made to him; and I cannot help flattering myself that, by your able management, with the assistance of those who act with you, the event of the two fleets holding Toulon, which under other circumstances might have created jealousy, may now be made the ground of a lasting and almost indissoluble connection between Spain and England. Lord Hood has conducted himself with infinite prudence, judgment and ability towards the Spaniards.

As I have no means of knowing the extent to which you may have authorized any interference in the arrangement of the French Government, I have cautiously avoided any appearance of directing or conducting any of their civil and political arrangements here, in which the Committee of Safety are perpetually requesting my interference or advice, I confine myself entirely within the line of military command for the defence of the place, in which I am obliged to be very positive; for, should I listen to suggestions, advice or remonstrances, public safety would soon be sacrificed to the object of sparing or covering private property.

I have divided the small parcels of Regs. which have been landed into two Batns. under the two senior captains, Capt. Moncrieff (a very able and active officer) of the 4th Regt., and Capt. Brereton of the 30th Regt. Don Gravina's accommodating disposition has induced him to propose that these captains should for the present take the *tour* of duty as officers of the day with the Spanish field officers, which I have readily accepted, as I feel great satisfaction and comfort in having British troops and officers as much mixed as possible in every point of our defence. The service absolutely required that I shd. appoint a Major of Brigade for the detail of duties between the two nations, to whom I hope the ordinary pay will be allowed. I have not applied for this in my official letter to Dundas, because my appointment is a matter of expediency and not an act of authority. I shall take the best precautions I can not to get the troops committed to my care into any scrape; but if the reinforcements arrive soon, I trust and hope I shall be able to take Marseilles and to keep it.

(Private.)

Toulon, September 24.

My dear Dundas,

Mulgrave trusts that the Brevet rank of Major will be conferred on Capts. Moncrieff and Brereton.

"I have touched as lightly as possible in my official letter to you upon the conduct of the Spaniards, but I am sorry to say that I feel but little confidence either in the skill of their officers or in the steadiness of their soldiers from anything I have seen of them. Several of them gave way at the commencement of the little action at la Grasse, and were driven back by some officers of the Navy who were on shore with a working party. Don Gravina, however, is a very fine fellow, and it is impossible for any persons to act with more perfect cordiality and good understanding than we do; but my distrust of the Spaniards obliges me to put a large proportion of British troops into all the Posts, which exposes them to very great fatigue; they bear it, however, with the utmost alacrity; and I trust to their spirit and firmness to prevent any panic which might occasion the loss of any of our western forts, the whole of which are unfinished, though they all have been considerably strengthened. Some of them indeed were barely traced out when I first came: there were guns in none, and it was not until yesterday that I have been able to put a battery of four 24 prs. into the important post of the Grand St Antoine which was before defended by musketry only. The first reinforcements will give us rest; in the meantime Gravina and I are always among the Posts; and if my despatches are incorrect and incomplete you will excuse it, as they are taken from my hours of sleep.

The enemy have been all day working at a battery at les Moulins; but we command them so much from la Grasse that they can do nothing."

P.S. 26th. *"My friend*, Genl. de Vins, has written to me a Jesuitical letter about sending troops; for I know from himself that his Instructions from his Court (which he showed me for a different object) were to satisfy the English in everything. The fact is that he wishes to have the credit of relieving Toulon himself if he succeeds in his operations; and upon this selfish idea he wishes to leave us to scramble for ourselves as well as we can, very indifferent to the success of the war if he can ensure the success of his own immediate operations: he certainly is an able officer; but I do not think as highly of his frankness and sincerity as I did before his professions were put to the trial. He must have been aware, as I have hinted to him in my letter, that nothing would have given so real effect to the operations on the side of Nice, as a vigorous manœûvre on the side of Toulon; for which object he ought to have sent us six or seven thousand men; but then the whole business would not have been done by himself; whereas if he drives the enemy back now, he drives them upon us; but we shall be ready for them. The last reports of deserters state la Bar and Carteaux together at 16000 men. Carteaux draws numbers from Marseilles by accounts of pretended advantages obtained against Toulon and promises of plunder. The rains have begun today. The enemy will, I think, suffer more from them than we shall; and I think they will be starved and soaked away before we are in sufficient force to attack them. At all events I will take good care of what we have before I attempt any offensive operations: there is nothing worth any hazard of being touch'd here."

(Private.)

My dear Dundas,   Toulon, October 3 (rec. November 14)[1].

I have treated the Spaniards as tenderly as possible in my public letter; the fact is they are good for nothing, officers and men, the only two fine fellows amongst them are their Sea General [Gravina] and their Marine sergt. [Moreno] mentioned in my letter—the first by the bye is a Sicilian....A board of Officers of Rank has been demanded to make enquiry into the shameful abandonment of the Post of Faron and to report whether they find grounds for demanding the judgment of a Court Martial. The Neapolitans are the finest looking troops I ever saw; not one of their officers or soldiers having ever seen a shot fired, I placed them in the least exposed part of an undertaking where there was little safety to offer to any one; they behaved with the steadiness of old troops, and after this first success in their

---

[1] Note the long delay in the receipt of Mulgrave's all important "private" letter.

maiden attack I have no doubt of their behaving like good and gallant troops on all occasion. The active intrepidity and steady firmness of the Piedmontese troops was equal to anything I ever saw; and I should think your Sardinian bargain a most excellent one indeed if they should be able to furnish 20,000 such troops as I have here; but I fear we must not rely as much upon their numbers, as I am convinced we may upon their good conduct and upon the real desire of the King of Sardinia to fulfill if possible his part of the treaty. I have thought it right to give you this little detail of the properties of our Allies at this place. Of the British I say nothing; you hear the same story that I should tell of them by your couriers from all quarters of the world.

P.S. We expect in a very few days to receive 1200 British troops with Gen. O'Hara from Gibraltar. Poor Gravina's wound makes the Spaniards very troublesome and difficult to manage; O'Hara's rank will make all management unnecessary.

Oct. 6th. I am sorry to open this letter again to tell you that I have received the most distressing accounts of the extreme terror and dismay of the Neapolitan troops posted on the height of Faron. Officers and soldiers make so little secret of their unexampled agitation and horror at being on an outpost that a single shot fired in the night would be sufficient to put them in confusion and rout, and again lose that Post. It is necessary to have numbers there to prevent the enemy attempting anything more. The Neapolitans shall be put under cover and the Piedmontese and British placed forwards. Every precaution I can take shall be taken. I say nothing in my public letter that may discourage the Neapolitans or alarm our people at Home; but I hope this will be preserved by you for my justification in case any misfortune should happen.

(Private.)

Toulon, October 18.

Dear Dundas,

Mulgrave describes the Spaniards' jealousy of command and their sending out a high officer to secure it; he suggests that to thwart their plan, the Duke of Gloucester be sent out, with an officer to advise him.... "Had the British troops led the column on October 15 [at Cape Brun] we should have been in possession of la Garde full half an hour before the enemy could arrive there; and all the deserters who have since come in have unanimously declared that, had they found us in la Garde, 1500 men would have surrendered and have delivered the Convention deputies into our hands, from an idea which the army had conceived that they had been marched out to be betrayed and cut off.... I have however shown no discontent to the Spaniards, who erred rather from sloth and ignorance than from any disinclination.... Poor Gravina's wound has been a very unfortunate circumstance for the service."

Dear Dundas,   Toulon, October 24.

Mulgrave declines his offer of a high post at Toulon.... "As Major-General Dundas and Major-General White are coming to assist General O'Hara, a fourth in command would be superfluous and unemployed with our small force. I shall therefore retire and render the best service in my power by giving such details as may be required of me.... Lord Hood will have given you a detail of the circumstances attending the extraordinary assumption and exercize of power by the Court of Spain in the appointment of a commander-in-chief of the combined forces, independent of a separate appointment of an officer to command the Spanish troops. I before gave you notice of the probability of the Spaniards exerting themselves by every means possible to keep a senior officer of their nation upon the spot; but I confess I was somewhat surprised when I found their object brought forward in so undisguised and unconciliatory a shape. Admiral Gravina has received the rank of Vice Admiral with the commission of commander-in-chief (Lt General) of the combined forces at Toulon. The amiable qualities and personal popularity of Gravina, which probably gave them hopes that this strange measure would not be resisted, serve only to render the measure more irksome and odious, from the necessity it creates of opposing and distressing a man for whom every individual of every nation composing a part of this army entertain the highest esteem. It is of the utmost importance that Lord Hood shd. have a flag at the main topmast head, with the commission dated even as far back as the capture of Toulon, or at least to the date when Conway came away, to prevent disputes afloat similar to that which has this day commenced on shore, or rather, relative to the land service; for the correspondence about this command in chief is carried on between Ld. Hood and Admiral Langara." He urges a reinforcement of good steady troops; "for the Spanish and Italian troops tend more to the reduction of the town by famine than to the defence of it by arms."

INDEX

Note. For names of ships mentioned throughout the text, see under the heading "Vessels."

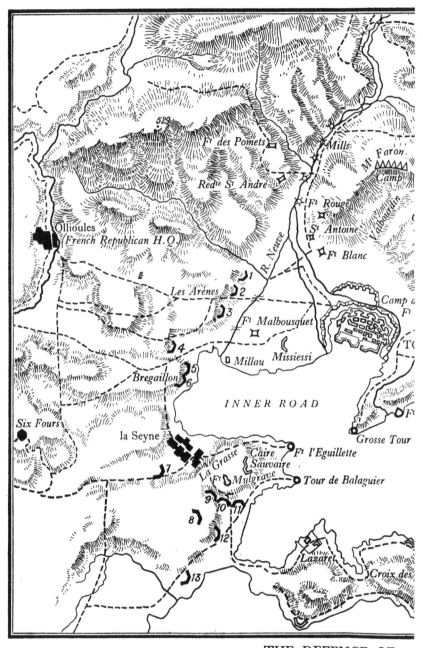

THE DEFENCE OF

Allied positions are marked in outline, those of the

French Republican Batteries:—1 Convention. 2 Farinière. 3 Poudrière.
8 Grande Rade. 9 Jacobins. 10 Hommes-sans-Peur.

TOULON, 1793

French Republican Army in solid black.

4 Rade. 5 Montagne. 6 Sans-Culottes. 7 Quatre Moulins.
11 Chasse-coquins. 12 Sablettes. 13 Faubrégas.

For EU product safety concerns, contact us at Calle de José Abascal, 56–1°,
28003 Madrid, Spain or eugpsr@cambridge.org.

www.ingramcontent.com/pod-product-compliance
Ingram Content Group UK Ltd.
Pitfield, Milton Keynes, MK11 3LW, UK
UKHW010047140625
459647UK00012BB/1670